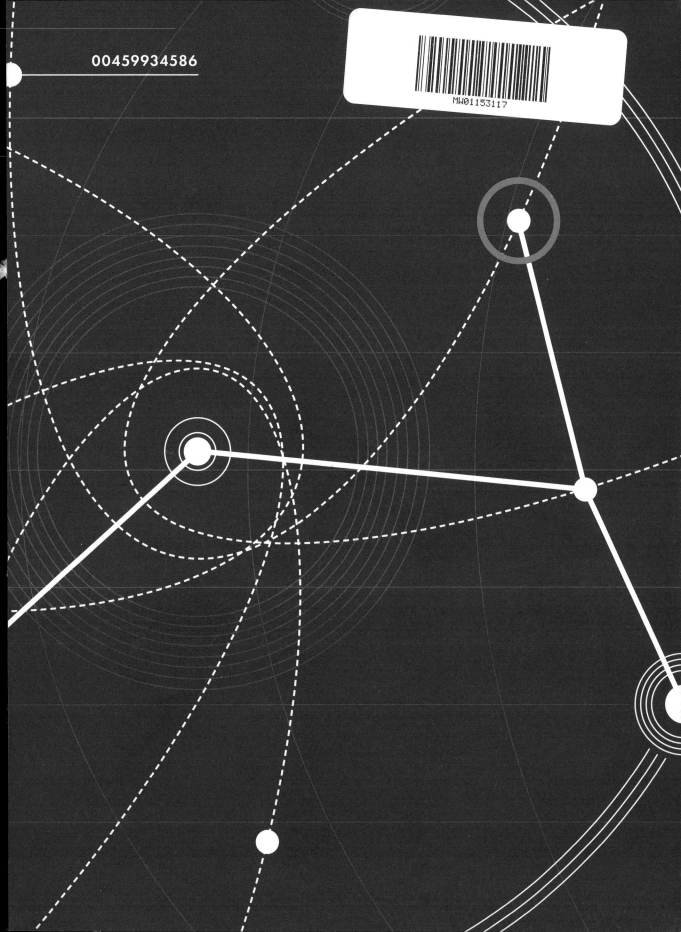

00459934586

MW01153117

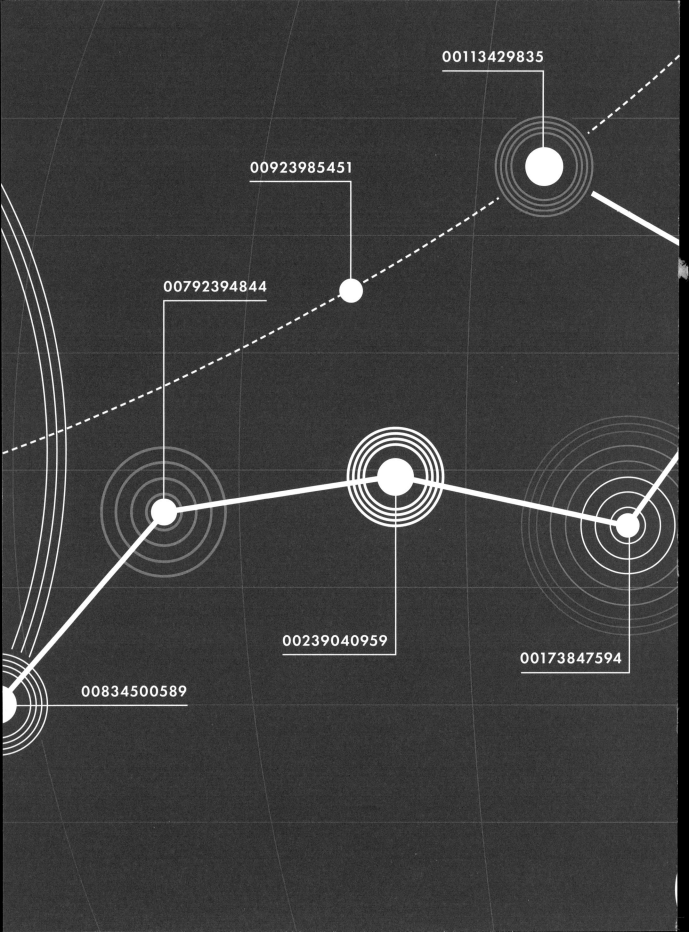

00113429835

00923985451

00792394844

00239040959

00173847594

00834500589

THE COMMISSION
PARADOX PROTOCOLS

THE COMMISSION PARADOX PROTOCOLS

A Complete Commission Guide to Temporal Anomalies

By Auggie Fletcher

ABRAMS, NEW YORK

CONTENTS

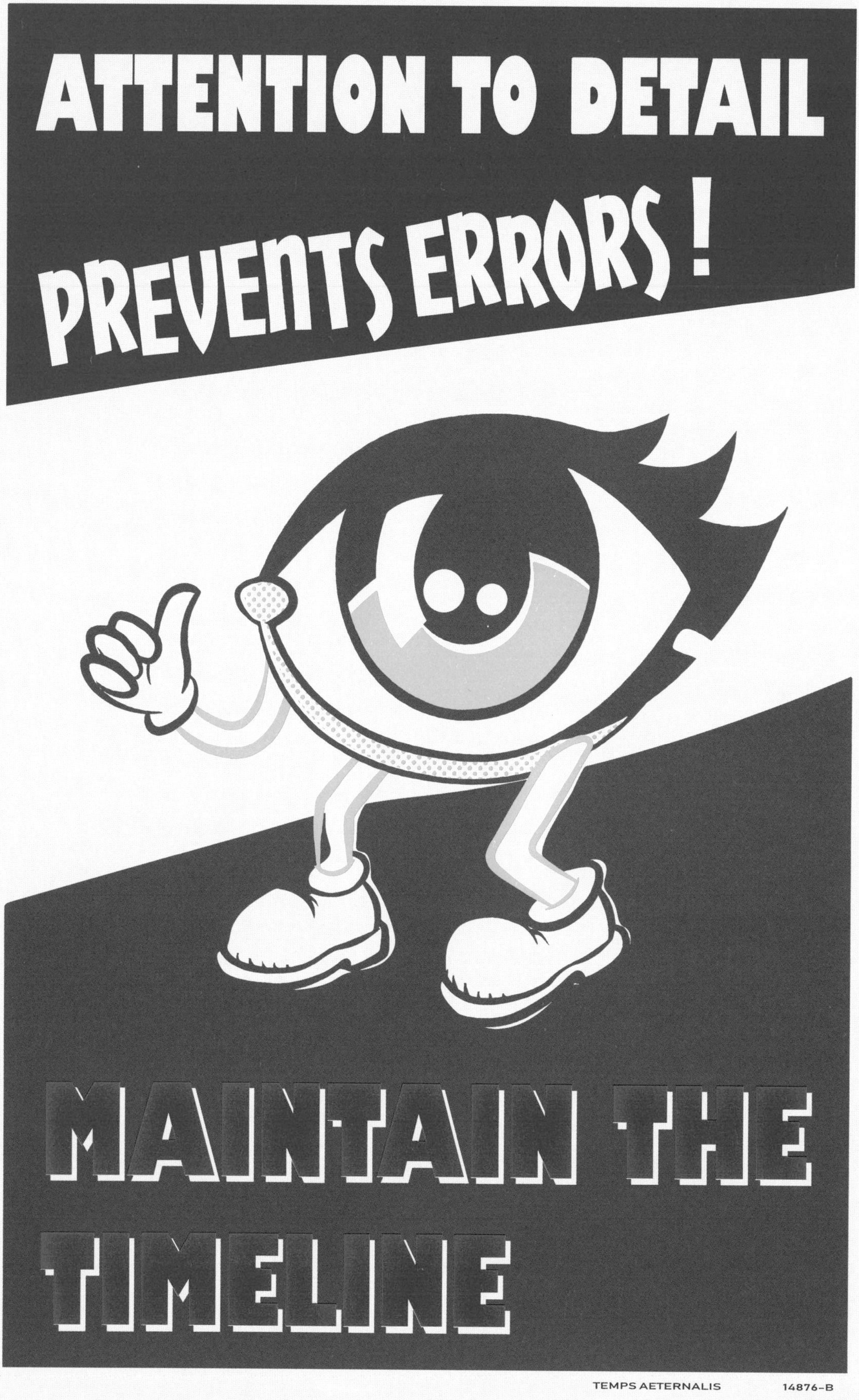
ATTENTION TO DETAIL
PREVENTS ERRORS!
MAINTAIN THE
TIMELINE

TEMPS AETERNALIS 14876-B

A FOREWORD FROM OUR FOUNDER

When I was asked to write a foreword for this book, my first thought was, *Why?* The Commission is as well-oiled a machine as you will find, and I, the Founder, don't do much more than sit in the passenger seat and enjoy the ride. But upon reflection, that's the point, isn't it? It's *you*; you are the reason we can do what we do here. You are reading my words because you are extraordinary; you are on the precipice of joining a select few who can truly say they save the world every day.

But how do we get there? How do we mold the future of our organization? We teach, we pass down knowledge, we learn from each other. We put ourselves in harm's way for the greater good, and we can do so because we're prepared. Many have asked why I created the Commission, and I have always been hesitant to answer. Sometimes it can feel safer to lead from the shadows, where your decisions can't be questioned. But there's no need for hesitancy here. Why should you devote your life to a cause that you cannot fully comprehend?

I created the Commission to fix a universe that was constantly breaking, careening off course into oblivion. I did so because it was necessary. Living is the only thing we truly ever do as human beings. And I made it my life's mission to make sure that continues to be the case. This handbook will teach you everything you need to know about the Commission. You'll learn about our tech, our business practices, and how we defy reality to make the world a better place.

With that said, the undeniable truth is that by receiving this book, by joining me on this journey, you have already accomplished so much. So, before you begin, I leave you with this:

Thank you.

THE COMMISSION ONLY *WORKS* WHEN *YOU* DO!

INTRODUCTION

Feel free to

Well, I suppose it would be appropriate to start this book with an introduction. <u>While I would prefer to remain nameless,</u> I've been asked to write a little about myself as a way to aid you in your learning process.

My name is Auggie Fletcher, and of the many important, world-altering jobs at the Commission, I have been tasked with the least important one:

You think quite highly of yourself, don't you?

~~Writing this book.~~ *Delete*

That's not to say I find this book to be meaningless. It certainly has merit, and I will give it the respect it deserves. Even so, <u>when you were born to fly,</u> it feels like a waste to teach others to do so from the ground. We are currently undergoing a bit of a "regime change" here at the Commission, so this book is meant to symbolize a new era for us. With that said, I ~~doubt most of~~ my dry wit will make it past my overbearing supervisor, Margot Archfield. *!*

Margot here... Make it past me?! Auggie you sub-mitted this without my final approval. My notes will contain the wrath of an editor scorned.

Throughout this book, I will provide my opinion on the things the higher-ups would prefer I present plainly. I will tell stories about employees that have been lost to the sands of time, and chiefly, I will tell the truth—<u>warts and all.</u> A Commission member must be prepared for everything, and thus, I will not pull any punches. When you put this book down, you'll be ready to join this crazy family. You are welcome in advance.

Worrying

From the outside looking in, it may seem reasonable to expect every distinct role at the Commission to function together seamlessly, for everything to work in lockstep at all times. That is not the case.

Amen

It's impossible for everyone to be aware of everything that goes on here, <u>such is the curse of bureaucracy.</u> It disturbed me how the roles were siloed when presented during my introduction. In a job where everything needs to be flawless and correct the first time, it's concerning that my education left much to be desired. I hope to create a synergy between every member of the Commission. No more back-room deals, office politics, or agents sent to an early grave. With this book, I've been given the opportunity to educate the next generation to create a safer and more reputable Commission.

When one of us fails, we all do. As a new member, it's paramount that you know the basics of every single job you could receive here, and every tool you'll have at your disposal. This knowledge may just save your life . . . or better yet, someone else's.

THE COMMISSION AND YOU: FINDING YOUR PLACE

SPECIAL OPS

Chances are, if you're reading this you've imagined yourself in the field, "fighting the good fight." And let's admit it, Special Ops are the cool kids. The kind who threw late-night keggers and didn't need to attend class because their parents had a wink-wink deal with the teachers.

I can feel the jealousy emanating off the page …

Unfortunately for them, our profession is a little more intense than a homecoming dance. And by that, I mean the mortality rate is obscenely high. Let's be specific here. 19.2 percent of Special Ops recruits will perish within their first five years in the field. There are a plethora of causes, from vehicular accidents to drowning to vending machines, but canoodling with a civilian's spouse is the most common, accounting for a whopping 26 percent of all lost agents. What's far scarier than a jilted lover, however, is when we lose agents and hear nothing of what happened to them. <u>They could be anywhere or any time, stranded in an era they know nothing about</u>.

You almost sound happy with this. Revise your tone, these people serve our most perilous role and deserve respect.

In order to mitigate these statistics, Special Ops agents are always given a specific breakdown of their mission goals, their extraction points, and an arsenal of tools that could get them out of trouble, but sometimes it feels as if they'd rather go off book and play out their inner artist than get the job done.

FIG. 1 CAUSE OF DEATH FOR SPECIAL OPS AGENTS

41%	Other
26%	Marital Strife
17%	Attacking the Wrong Target
8%	Landing over the Sea
5%	Lost Briefcase
3%	Faulty Briefcase

I know I may seem like a grouch, and in truth I kind of am. Special Ops is the final part of the equation, but when they fail to swing their sword correctly, we all look bad. That's not to say there aren't Special Ops agents I respect. For example, an agent like Five is legendary not only because of his flashy abilities, but because he gets the job done. No excuses. No running off. Only efficiency. The goal of this book is to educate new recruits to follow suit, be direct and calculating. It's a near-impossible task for the type of people that typically find themselves in this role—nauseatingly self-interested and ready to go off script and take unnecessary risks. I'd like to curtail that. If I can help to reduce the mortality rate of new recruits and limit their tendency to deviate on missions and put both themselves and the timeline at risk, I will have done my job.

Despite my (warranted) criticism, Special Ops provides an extremely important function to the Commission. They are the proverbial knives that cut the meat (cooked to perfection and brought to them on a silver platter, but I digress).

Each Special Ops team is typically composed of two agents and is issued a company-approved briefcase that will help them jump through time and make sure they are always ready for extraction. Depending on the location of their mission or their likelihood to cross paths with a member of the Umbrella or Sparrow Academies, they may also be equipped with specialized tools that will be covered in a later chapter.

Could have fooled me...

You finally make some sense here, more of this!

Auggie, your whiny tone here is lost on me. These are the people who risk their lives to keep things running smoothly here. Revise in future editions.

The ideal Special Ops candidate must be brave and willing to make hard choices under pressure. They must be able to acclimate to new environments quickly and carry out orders they may not understand. Lastly, and this is a requirement for the role, they must be willing to kill at a moment's notice, no matter who, what, why, or when, in order to preserve the proper timeline.

Let's not under-sell their need to kill, please.

But let's get more technical. There is a massive misconception that flies around about Special Ops, and I'm here to set the record straight. It'd be easy to assume that a well-trained agent is essentially a glorified assassin, but that couldn't be further from the truth. While it is true that a large number of Special Ops missions involve eliminating a target, an agent can just as easily be sent to tip over a cow or steal candy from a baby. The point is that agents are supposed to impact the timeline in extremely specific ways, and it just so happens that a shot to the head is often the best way of solving that problem.

From your mouth to the Founder's ears!

The problems tend to come to the forefront when an agent is assigned a task that they feel is beneath them. Imagine if we asked Babe Ruth to play T-ball—I'm sure he wouldn't be happy either. So, when an agent with twenty-six kills to their name is asked to deliver a birthday cake to a Chuck E. Cheese . . . Well, that's when they typically act out and things go off the rails.

In training, we try to impress upon young recruits that their job is simply to carry out tasks: no more, no less. In order to fully communicate this to our recruits, they are put through simple drills like opening the door for the Handler, fetching the Handler's mail, and doing the Handler's laundry. Throughout the rigorous itinerary, many recruits question why they're being forced through what they define as a "slog," and the Handler calmly explains that they are simply one part of a long chain—a means to an end—and if they don't learn to get the small stuff right, how can they tackle entire governments? Shockingly, this pep talk actually does seem to inspire some agents (ever the masochists). In reality, the Handler just needs a ton of help in her personal life.

Feels like you're making this up; excessive.

Like her gumption

Here I provide a concise profile of a typical Special Ops agent. I hope this gives you recruits an idea of where you may best fit in at the commission.

PROFILE: SPECIAL OPS – ROBERT KINGSLEY

"By any means necessary"

Successful missions: **42**
Success rate: **83%**
Civilian casualties: **132**
Conscience: **Clear**
High school clique: **Jock**
Favorite movie: *Scarface*

ATTRIBUTES
- Aggressive
- Traveler
- Problem-solver
- Killer work ethic

GOALS
- Terminate targets
- Restore the timeline
- Return home alive

FRUSTRATIONS
- The Umbrella and Sparrow Academies
- Do-gooders
- Identical twins

TECHNOLOGY
- Briefcase
- Porcupine spikes laced with poison

BIO
Robert Kingsley is about as clean as it gets for a Special Ops agent. A success rate of 83 percent is almost unheard of, and with only 132 civilian casualties, he has left a relatively limited amount of stress on the timeline. Robert's favored weapon to use is a small porcupine named Porky. When attempting to terminate a target, Robert will ask them if they want to hold his porcupine, and everything falls into place from there. He's nonthreatening, which makes his job slightly easier as adversaries don't see him as a threat until it's too late.

PERSONALITY

INTROVERT	·················⋈·····	EXTROVERT
INTUITIVE	········⋈·············	SENSING
THINKING	··············⋈····	FEELING
JUDGING	······⋈··············	PERCEIVING

GROUNDBREAKING TECH

Everybody wants to know about our tech, because of course they do. It's what sets us apart from everyone else. There's a good reason for that. Commission agents are regular people at their core. They may be skilled fighters or genius tacticians, but they still put their pants on one leg at a time. We rely on our tech to turn the ordinary man or woman into an extraordinary force.

We can talk them up more, they are our heroes.

~~Now you may be thinking that there's something funny going on here, that we're able to do what we do because of magic, or God, or something else.~~ I assure you that there is nothing of the sort going on. Everything we do is scientifically backed because only science—and nothing else—can be trusted 100 percent of the time.

delete

For Special Ops, the choice of tech to utilize to achieve their goals is a no-brainer.

BRIEFCASE

What did this woman do to you?

You can't talk about Special Ops without talking about the briefcase. The two go hand in hand, like peanut butter and jelly or the Handler and three-hour lunches. Every Special Ops agent is sent into the field equipped with this truly miraculous piece of technology. It can stop time, travel through it, and heck, it's even stylish. But how does it work? Here's the secret . . . I don't know.

Kidding! In the early days of training, there was a worry that some of our concepts would be too difficult to parse for new recruits and lead to them never truly understanding the power someone in their position holds. Therefore, it was decided that we should utilize mascots to (in their words) "dumb things down for the newbies." That's how we got this abomination:

Mr. Briefcase was created to be an avatar for our previous leadership, a friendly presence and a goofy visage that was ultimately extremely unhelpful. Mr. Briefcase be-

Mr. Briefcase is a national treasure!! I will not tolerate this slander.

came the go-to when anyone asked for an explanation of how any of this stuff worked. If any recruit was unsure about something, they were referred to a 540-second video starring Mr. Briefcase that claimed to be the ultimate resource for education here at the Commission.

And it is! Surely you're not doubting our higher-ups.

The fact is, it was insufficient, and prior to this book, recruits simply did not have full knowledge of how anything here truly worked. They were race car drivers put in the cockpit of fighter jets. The results (as always with poorly made plans) were disastrous. ~~Countless agents were lost when their briefcase malfunctioned, and they had no real knowledge of how to get themselves home.~~

Conjecture. delete.

Forgive my tangent, all this is to say that time travel is extremely complicated. Any explanation of the tech we use is tough to convey without relying on the crutch of witty slogans and relatable cartoon characters. But as promised, I will try to explain.

Have you ever heard of the term Occam's razor? That sometimes when only the simplest explanation can be true, then it must be? Well, somebody must need to shave, because I have a razor right here.

Like Five, the Founder was able to master the ability to time travel. While Five uses his own body as a conduit, weak and unreliable, a briefcase is tied to a computer, calculating and exact. When using a briefcase, you set the dials to the exact point in the timeline you want to go to, and just like that, you're off. No muss, no fuss, no coconuts. The dials are able to utilize the historical data gathered by the Infinite Switchboard in order to make every single jump exact. When something causes the dials to malfunction, like a stray bullet or an extra-saucy sandwich, the connection can be severed. This can cause the briefcase to send agents to unforeseen locations and time eras.

Do you actually know how the briefcase works, or are you just guessing? Sounds like you made it up; revise.

In short, the actual method of time traveling (when done correctly) is relatively easy. This makes it so important to learn the rules of what is and isn't acceptable to do as you traverse the timelines. Remember, tech doesn't cause our problems—misuse of it does.

WORKPLACE HAZARDS

It may seem like I'm beating a dead horse now, but I'm going to take another swing: Time travel can be a cruel and unforgiving mistress. Even when every reasonable precaution is taken, the possibility for things to go awry remains high. This section will feature a breakdown of the common paradoxes Special Ops agents may experience in the field. With this knowledge, our hope is that you will be better prepared to hold our timeline together.

Predestination Paradox

No one really knows anything; it's the unbearable truth of the universe. We know what we're told and learn from those who were told by others. This massive game of telephone was how communication began. Word travels from mouth to mouth until legend becomes fact. Isn't that the beauty of our world; to know something to be true with all your heart until you realize you're wrong? The Earth was flat until it wasn't. The sun used to revolve around us, and we came from a rib in Adam's chest. Nothing would be fun if it was always simple and straightforward. There's always more to discover, to learn, especially here, where infinity is reality.

Get to the point.

That brings us to <u>Cassidy "The Tragedy" Cartwright</u>. Ask anyone at the Commission and they'll tell you that she is the worst field agent that we have ever seen, and if you only looked at the raw numbers, you'd be right. Cassidy had zero confirmed kills and never completed a single mission objective she was given. Objectively, by any rational measure, Cassidy was awful at her job. And boy did she hear about it. She'd receive constant ridicule at the Commission as coworkers went out of their way to humiliate her and call out her infamous record. Going so far as to hide her briefcase from her and bribe the woman in charge of sending messages through our tube system, Gloria, into sending her notes that the Commission was better off without her.

But I looked deeper. Cassidy was a high-end recruit. Hell, you could have written *The Natural* about her. So why was she so poor in the field? It didn't add up. So I kept digging. I used the password I had pulled from the Handler's files when I worked for her to get a peek at Cassidy's file. I learned that before she joined the Commission, Cassidy's son was killed as he tried to stop a mugger that attacked her. There was a fight for the gun. It went off, and the mugger went running and Cassidy was left to watch her son bleed out in front of her. It's noted that she sat there, his body limp over her knee, for four hours, muttering to herself, "I need to go back, I have to go back."

This obsession with going back, the desire to change the past for a better future, hit the Commission's radar like a freight train. Here was a woman now free from responsibility that was determined to fight the good fight.

What a steal! At least, that's what the nearsighted leeches on the Board must have thought. When she first arrived at the Commission, it's like she had received a new lease on life. No one studied harder or completely devoted themselves to our ethos quite like her. She wanted to be a field agent, and she made it near impossible for anyone to deny her that role.

Our muddied minds viewed her as a true believer in our ways. <u>"She's the best of us,"</u> people would say. But internally, she knew that absolutely everything she was doing was to achieve one goal: bring her son back.

Buckle in, folks...

You what?!?

Exaggeration

Eventually the hard work paid off, and she was given a mission. She was meant to terminate a flower merchant in order to trigger the attack on Pearl Harbor, but she didn't pay attention to a single word in her briefing. In truth, they could have told her to go anywhere and she would have nodded and smiled, said she understood however many times she needed to in order to get out of the room. There was only one place she was headed, a nearly empty back alley where her life had changed so long ago.

But as we've said, time travel is a tricky thing, as predictable as it is unpredictable. Cassidy likely knew the problem before she even left, but hell, it was worth a shot. Her son's death shattered her entire life, so who's to say the impossible couldn't strike twice? This brings us to the root of the Predestination Paradox, the law that states that returning to the past and attempting to change something that had led to you specifically being there will always yield the same result. In scientific terms, the "Timeline-Protection Hypothesis" states that any attempts to change the timeline would result in a probability distortion being created to protect the timeline. Furthermore, a highly improbable event may occur in order to prevent a paradoxical, impossible event from taking place. The timeline will literally fight to maintain itself.

The only way Cassidy could travel back to save her son is if she had watched him pass. Meaning, every time Cassidy traveled back to save her son, the outcome was always the same. She was always a step late, the gun would always go off, and she'd be left with the pain. Yet, every mission she was sent on, she would go back and try again and again and again. Until she was sent away from the Commission, an abject failure by any rational notion.

This is something I'm trying to get at through this handbook, something that will probably not make it to print. We exist in an extremely specific place in the universe. We have access to unlimited timelines. The world is at our fingertips at every moment, yet we are in a race to limit ourselves. Make ourselves think the same as everyone else to fit in, not questioning why we feel the way we do, when the one who convinced us also failed to do the same. It's a brutal cycle. The point is that we lost Cassidy Cartwright three years ago. She was a walking punch line and meant nothing to most people here. But not to me.

You're spending a lot of time on Cassidy that would be better spent elsewhere.

If I had a nickel for every mistake we've made, I'd be a billionaire, but the same can be said for our successes. Do you see what I mean? We play an infinite game here. Stop fixating on one loss.

FROM THE OFFICE OF THE FOUNDER

I met Cassidy when she was a new recruit. There was no one more focused than her; it was suggested by the Board that I meet her as an effort in our outreach to our younger stars. I saw something in her eyes that no one else saw: pain. So much pain. Cassidy and I understood each other.

We shared a common goal and devoted our lives to achieving it.

The treatment that Cassidy received from her coworkers was completely unacceptable. I tried to stop it, but sometimes I feel like Rapunzel, trapped in a large castle up on a hill, high enough so no one can hear me calling down. I wish I could have done more for her. She deserved more from me.

I think about her a lot in my quiet moments. She reminds me of how badly I want this crazy experiment to work. I want to go back desperately. I want to go back to a time where people like Cassidy didn't need to exist. Needlessly bashing their heads against the wall in the hopes that they can make a difference and change this world for their better. I conflate her with myself, if that much is not clear. She was smarter than I was, a harder worker, she cared more. And she still failed.

I don't want to think further on that point.

Thank you for this passage, Auggie.

Bootstrap Paradox

Now you're getting it

Not all stories about the Commission and time travel are emotional and heart-wrenching. <u>In fact, very few of them are.</u> You give extremely powerful people access to a device that effectively shelters them from any moral retribution from the universe and, well, things are going to get ugly.

Even before I was given the task of writing this book, I was worried about what happened when those we refer to as "playboy" agents found themselves in relations with people they came across during their travels. Unsurprisingly, the results are not only disastrous but depressingly frequent. Like a kid grabbing all the candy from a house that left an unattended bowl out for Halloween, some people can't help themselves. This leads us to the Bootstrap Paradox.

Let's break it down with help of vaunted physicist Albert Einstein, who's theories are regularly taught at the Commission as an introductory course. Einstein's theory of relativity tells us that we have got almost complete freedom of movement into the future. Time travel to the past, on the other hand, throws up a number of paradoxes. Great, we know that already. So let's get more granular. Imagine a scenario where a time traveler went back in time and taught Einstein the theory of relativity before returning to his own time. Einstein claims it's his own work, and over the following decades the theory is published countless times until a copy of it eventually ends up in the hands of the original time traveler, who then takes it back to Einstein, begging the question "where did the theory originate?" We cannot say that it came from the time traveler as he learned it from Einstein, but we also cannot say that it is from Einstein, since he was taught it by the time traveler. This creates a causal loop and results in the question: Who, then, discovered the theory of relativity? The answer is (1) we don't know, and (2) the timeline will suffer from its inability to provide an answer.

Unfortunately, I concur; maybe take this out. Don't want anyone getting ideas.

But how does this come into the equation for the Commission? Don't we always try to leave no trace? Unfortunately, some agents have found themselves rearing children on their missions, which is a massive problem. Essentially, if an agent has a child and then leaves the timeline, it means that one of the child's parents will have never existed, which puts great stress on the timeline. It's a strict Commission guideline that Special Ops should not fraternize with anyone while

~~completing their mission—under any circumstances. Unsurprisingly, this rule is at best ignored and at worst openly disobeyed.~~

Cut this as well

There's one agent who mocked this rule openly. He was good-looking, charismatic, undoubtedly a good hang. I mean, look, his name was Clinton West, and he wore it proudly. Clinton was a classic free-lancer—he'd get the mission done every time he was sent out, but he certainly would have a good time doing it. He'd hold court in our break rooms and tell stories of his conquests far and wide, but what he never did tell is that he would ask the women to carry his child to term no matter what. He'd promise money, power, whatever it took for them to agree. Then they would never see him again. This was Clinton's foolhardy way to leave a stamp on this world.

Could you imagine a more narcissistic coping mechanism?

Well, Clinton got greedy. He made it his mission to sleep with a woman from every decade of the twentieth century. And at first it went well. It seemed like he was throwing a perfect game. But everything changed when one of his "partners" in Australia gave birth to a young boy who mistreated an emu in 1932. The resulting fallout led to the bizarre and terrifying Emu Wars that <u>almost brought an entire conti-nent to its knees</u>. After the resulting fallout there was a crackdown, and Clinton was given a severance package and sent deep into the wilder-ness in Tasmania to fend for himself until nature could take its revenge. After that, <u>the Commission at least began to show some cojones</u> and began to change things. They began to shift away from the "partier" type they'd typically bring in and focused more on the determined serial-killer type. That's a joke! Just normal killers.

This feels like conjecture, refrain from this.

Thank you for the modicum of credit. Those who purposely choose to cause us headaches should be expunged from our organization.

Even so, the doctrine is still seen as overbearing by some here, a reminder that Mommy and Daddy have their watchful eye on you, and God forbid if you ever disobey them. What a shame, a group of people claiming paternalistic views from their superiors while not actually exam-ining why the doctrine was handed down in the first place. So please let me be unequivocally clear: The rules should be followed strictly in this case, with no exceptions. To leave a child without a parent is immoral, to say nothing about what it does to the timeline. At the Commission, we have a very explicit job in the world's ecosystem. <u>We are here to help keep the world on its axis, not apply our own tilt where we see fit.</u>

Rare instance where I will compliment your prose.

Grandfather Paradox

This handbook walks you through a myriad of problems and pitfalls to avoid, but there is one thing that must be avoided at all costs, as it leads to the breakdown of absolutely everything. It's the moment when the toothpaste is fully out of the tube: the Grandfather Paradox.

The Grandfather Paradox is the timeline's version of a closing bell, where everything falls in upon itself. It's similar to when your body feels sick and forces itself to throw up. It signals that something is wrong and you're in need of a full-on reset.

Let's talk about why. What is it about this paradox that it so violently dismantles a timeline? The term refers to a hypothetical situation where a person travels to a time before their grandfather had children and kills him, thus making their own birth impossible. But the Commission doesn't deal in hypotheticals. When your job covers every single possible outcome, the improbable tends to happen. So what happens next? Does everything combust? No, not initially.

Essentially, the rift causes an ever-growing *kugelblitz* that will consume and consume until the world folds in upon itself. As a Commission employee, your first move when you discover a *kugelblitz* is to retreat back to the Commission immediately—do not attempt to save anyone in the existing timeline as they are doomed. Upon returning to the Commission, you must report to the Founder immediately and he will give direction on how to move forward.

There are rumors about what the Founder tells those that come across a *kugelblitz*. Few have experienced the phenomenon, and those who have survived aren't necessarily the chattiest bunch. The prevailing theory is that a *kugelblitz* is a natural end to our time-travel anomalies. In a future section, I will show you the flowcharts Analysts use to calculate their changes, and you will begin to comprehend what it means for a timeline to splinter off.

It's true what they say, the universe *is* endlessly expanding, but what isn't mentioned is that it shrinks at the same time. As new timelines emerge, there are those that will eventually succumb to the Grandfather Paradox, which will give way to the *kugelblitz* that will then lead to a universe that can no longer exist. Yin and yang.

This, of course, is all hypothetical, but it all tracks for me. All we do here is try our best to minimize the splinters, dive into the water like

Yes, Auggie, the collapse of a time line is comparable to drinking too much peppermint schnapps.

Please cite evidence

a pencil instead of a boisterous cannonball, to keep things calm. We try to limit the expansion because we know it will end in worlds being created that will one day collapse upon themselves. When we mess about while correcting the past, <u>universes burn.</u>

This chapter has made me consider what kind of guy the Founder is. I've never met him—most of us haven't—and those who have tend to stay silent about their interaction. Is he an optimist? It just feels as if we're playing a losing game here. And when we lose, we lose big every time. I wonder if he's aware of that. If he knew that trying to save one world would ruin so many others.

I think back to Five, how he's the only individual to rival the Commission's power. I wonder if perhaps the Commission and Five were more intertwined than we first thought. Excuse me if this type of theorizing is out of place, but here we are taught how to question things and piece together how they work. That's all I'm doing.

What if Five did exist in an original timeline that was pure? But he traveled back in time to save someone or someone's life (we already know that Five will go to great lengths for his family). In doing so, he created fractures in his original timeline. The splits led to alternate paths, paths that someday lead to the eventual destruction of their universes. An endless cycle of perpetual death. But maybe Five clocked this and fully understood the fallout of his decision.

It would follow that this original Five may have used his powers to create the Commission, an organization that was focused on putting the toothpaste back into the tube, to returning everything to the way it was in an attempt to bring their timeline closer to the original.

Pulling this off would be the equivalent of asking someone to cross the Pacific Ocean with a blindfold on and a shark on their tail. It's impossible. In truth, I can admit that what we're doing is impossible. I know this isn't a great recruiting tool and should be omitted from this handbook, but we are fighting a losing battle, one we may never win. But it's worth it because every ripple we can limit in a timeline means trillions of lives saved. For us, the battle is worth it. Even if we know we won't win the war, we're doing the impossible and asking for a little more help to keep it going.

Jeez, Auggie

Too negative

Just this once I will show you how a real section should be written and take a literal page out of your predecessor's edition. →
If your future writing does not reflect the standard set here, then rest assured you will not continue this project.

CHAPTER LXVIII

THE GRANDFATHER PARADOX

INTRODUCTION

Temporal anomalies have existed since the very beginning of time itself. The birth of the Commission is what has allowed us to understand and further research inconsistencies that can (and do) occur in the timeline. However, before we were able to use our own methods to manipulate time, we must explore the origin of temporal anomalies. The existence of temporal anomalies, and the knowledge of such, is deeply rooted in the spiritual tradition of human history.

Oral tradition over the centuries has given us access to stories that indicate people who have known about these anomalies. Early societies often categorized these people as religious or spiritual, since they claimed they were able to see the future. In reality, their ability to predict certain events stemmed from the fact that they were gifted with the abilities to time travel. Instead of actually being clairvoyant, these people were merely able to do what we do in The Commission today. the Commission is where we were able to harness and organize this power into one place of control.

However, the actual anomalies themselves came from these people not understanding their jobs, and perhaps moving into a different timeline that they are not permitted in. Often, matters of the heart have been the greatest offender of all in these cases. A poor soul's

emotions would get the best of them, causing them to make a decision that does not fit into the correct timeline. Thus, disaster would ensue. As civilisation has progressed, we have been able to control these errors in causal time loops, which has almost banished the reign of chaos in our world. Now, the perfectly structured institution that is the Commission has almost wholly eradicated the existence of temporal anomalies. If one does happen to occur, this guide shall outline the best way to fix the chaos that one has created.

THEORY

Some of the earliest examples of temporal anomalies can be seen in the most famous events in human history. Arguably one of the most famous events in history is the death and the resurrection of Jesus Christ. Although popular Christian mythology has explained the resurrection of Jesus after 3 days of death to a 'God', any Commission employee knows that Jesus Christ was merely a temporal anomaly – his death was not supposed to occur in that timeline, which forced him to attempt to fix this by coming back to life.

This may be one of the most royal screwups of Commission history (however, we must add that this was before the current management stepped in). It is quite depressing to see the way that religious extremists have taken this misstep

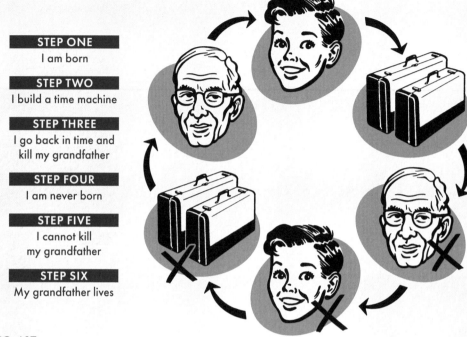

STEP ONE
I am born

STEP TWO
I build a time machine

STEP THREE
I go back in time and kill my grandfather

STEP FOUR
I am never born

STEP FIVE
I cannot kill my grandfather

STEP SIX
My grandfather lives

FIG. 607

in the timeline as fodder for conflict and wars throughout centuries, and hence why we are vigilant in our work to prevent such errors.

Here at the Commission, we take our anomaly prevention work very seriously. It is imperative that any person wishing to avoid any and all temporal anomalies take steps to set themselves up for the utmost success in this endeavor. This dossier will serve as an instruction handbook, or rather a survival guide of sorts, on this exact topic. In order to prevent the most egregious anomaly of all, which is known as the Grandfather Complex, one must be vigilant in their time travel and always aware of the ways in which their action could be completely changing the future events of any given timeline. As we see played out in the 2008 major motion picture *Sliding Doors*, starring Goop-extraordinaire Gwyneth Paltrow, any wrong action taken can have completely disastrous effects.

In order to prevent a Grandfather Paradox, one must make sure that everything happens according to plan when it comes to those who survive and those who pass away. Because, if someone who is supposed to die is saved, or alternatively, if they die, they could go on to cause a Grandfather Complex. We can define this term as such: The Grandfather Paradox is a potential logical problem that would arise if a person were to travel to a past time. The name comes from the idea that if a person travels to a time before their grandfather had children, and kills him, it would make their own birth impossible. That is why the number-one rule in temporal anomaly prevention is that said time traveller must have complete and utter control of one's emotions – or rather, be able to exist without much emotion at all. In the past, the birth of a Grandfather Paradox has usually come from a commission employee's heart getting in the way of their task.

PROTOCOL

In the unlikely case of the Grandfather Paradox, the Founder and any essential personnel should be immediately remanded to the operations bunker.

The Grandfather Paradox may involve the overlapping of timelines within the universe. These timelines may run parallel or concurrent with each other. For further reading on this subject please refer to the manual addendum twenty-two on timeline overlap and related protocols.

WARNINGS & SIDE EFFECTS

Doppelgängers – the occurrence of doppelgängers, while initially fascinating, is a grave and serious indication of trouble and must be avoided at all costs. Doppelgängers may include two identical beings, human or otherwise, from different timelines, but the list extends to inanimate objects imbued with human or creature memories, such as photographs, keepsakes, furniture, clothing and other soft goods. If you observe any object spontaneously combust, it is recommended, out of an abundance of caution, that you check in with headquarters to confirm or deny the occurrence of a Grandfather Paradox. The situation changes drastically with human doppelgängers. When two human doppelgänger subjects are within close proximity, an unmistakable list of symptoms, including itching, swelling and hives, will undoubtedly make its presence known in all places but the operations bunker. However, if the two subjects are not removed from each other's proximity quickly enough, it is likely that one or both subjects will suffer from paradox psychosis.

Paradox Psychosis – a potentially lethal condition onset by a number of factors pertaining to the occurrence of one or many paradoxes. Symptoms are exacerbated when opposing, identical or contradictory forces are in close proximity to each other. Beware doppelgängers, instances of déjà vu, irregular sleep patterns and/or unexplained fatigue. Symptoms include rash, itching, burning, delusions, and in accelerated cases, aggressive behavior, confusion, delirium and possibly death. The Grandfather Paradox is especially vulnerable to paradox psychosis, as any overlap, random or otherwise, will be affected and likely destroyed. However, it is your duty to find these anomalies and bring them in for observation. As always, if you, the Founder or any of your colleagues begins suffering from Paradox Psychosis, you are required to report it to HR immediately, even if you are not aware of any current paradox occurring. Remember, if you or a colleague is suffering from advanced paradox psychosis, the Commission officially recommends terminating one or both overlapping entities in favor of preserving the paradox's status quo. While at times random and seemingly cruel, paradox psychosis is a serious threat to the already precarious situation that a Grandfather Paradox presents and if not dealt with immediately, can contribute to an accelerated unraveling of the universe, and vast civilian casualties across multiple timelines.

Paradox Psychosis

In previous editions of the handbook, Paradox Psychosis could be found in Chapter 27, Subsection 3b, but it often went overlooked, so I've opted to define it here. By this point, everybody and their mother knows what Paradox Psychosis is, but I'm a generous man, and by definition, the purpose of this book is to educate the uninitiated, so here goes nothing.

Boy, I'm still thinking about how good I did on the last section.

no way!

The first thing to understand is what I've been trying to drill into your head throughout this entire book. Time travel is downright tricky, and converging timelines are an absolutely unavoidable problem in our line of work. We're like plumbers who try to fix a leak in your sink but then turn every toilet into an erupting fire hydrant. Point being, there is always fallout from what we do, and though we try to minimize our influence, accidents happen even when everything has technically gone properly. So here's how to first identify Paradox Psychosis, properly diagnose it, and then, most importantly, combat it. *Good*

The first thing to keep your eye out for is the doppelgängers, which is more complicated than it sounds. We live in a world with identical twins, you might say. Doesn't that make this nearly impossible? And the answer is yes, but it's actually harder than that. For instance, doppelgängers may not be the same age. Imagine a six-year-old version of yourself passing you in the present day—would you even notice?

Luckily, the Infinite Switchboard will flag these encounters as anomalies. A talented operator should be able to help identify which people spawned this anomaly. Only once in history have three doppelgängers been located in a nearby proximity. It was weirdly celebrated here, and we even popped champagne. Oh well, I guess when so much of your life is spent swimming upstream, you need to celebrate the small moments.

Do we need to?

What's more complicated is that the idea of doppelgängers isn't limited to humans—the universe does not, in fact, revolve only around us. Photographs, keepsakes, furniture, clothing, and other items can all cross timelines. They are harder to find than human doppelgängers but are thankfully much less harmful. They may themselves combust, but outside of that, large-scale problems are unlikely. When two humans are in close proximity for a considerable amount of time, they will begin exhibiting the symptoms for Paradox Psychosis.

Can we stay focused on the timelines and how they affect people?

1. Denial

Very introspective

This one is fairly obvious. The first reaction when two human doppel-gängers come into contact with each other is denial, and why wouldn't it be? <u>Nobody wants to believe that another version of themselves could exist in the world, and even the suggestion can shatter some-one's entire world.</u> So while this is absolutely a normal reaction to this scenario, when coupled with the following symptoms, it is absolutely a harbinger of Paradox Psychosis.

2. Itching

Next up is itching, which may initially sound harmless, but the type we're discussing here is an almost violent form of self-harm, tearing at the body's skin until it begins to erode. Once you see someone manically going after their own skin while repeatedly denying the existence of their doppelgänger, they become a surefire candidate for Paradox Psychosis.

3. Extreme Thirst and Urination

At this point, you should be able to pinpoint someone undergoing Paradox Psychosis, but it's important to work through the list of symptoms to completely free yourself from doubt. At stage three, the subject will demand water, trying to fill an insatiable thirst. At the same time, they will begin to need to use the bathroom almost constantly, turning their body into a walking, talking funnel. This shows how loose their grip on the world is, as they are essentially unable to retain any matter.

That's me after chili day at the Commission deli...

4. Excessive Gas

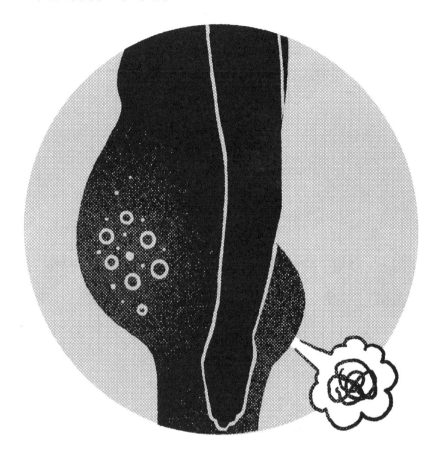

While excessive gas has certainly been associated with Paradox Psychosis, <u>there is not much tangible evidence</u> that it should be included as a symptom. Essentially, it's an issue of correlation vs. causation. But look, it must be said that these symptoms have been approved by the Founder, so we're working with this knowledge from the top down. Unless our Founder is a massive prankster, extreme flatulence should be considered a viable identifier for Paradox Psychosis.

Must you question everything?

5. Acute Paranoia

This is when the true panic sets in and subjects begin to interrogate their own lives and everyone around them. If another version of themselves exists, then what else is a lie? They begin to hear murmurs from random passersby, anyone so much as within earshot. They will also begin rambling on about their doppelgänger, accusing them of stealing their identity and ultimately working to guarantee their demise. It's in this stage that the peril of Paradox Psychosis sets in, the idea that only one of them must live in order to ensure a balanced universe will firmly take hold.

6. Uncontrolled Perspiration

In a last act of rebellion, the subject's body will begin secreting sweat at an alarming rate. This shows that the subject has completely lost control of their bodily functions and is operating on pure instinct alone. The subject will not even attempt to pat themselves dry, and they are nonplussed when a loved one asks them what is going on. Their eyes will begin darting around the room, searching for their doppelgänger so they can enact their final symptom, which unfortunately is . . .

7. Homicidal Rage

When the subject has progressed through all symptoms, they will begin to devise plans to accomplish something they find to be an absolute necessity: eliminate their doppelgänger. It's unfortunately a fairly natural conclusion. Everything was fine before they came along and now this person represents the crumbling of their entire world. Subjects will stop at nothing until this goal is accomplished. They will bribe people and act in ways that previously would have been considered unimaginable. The sad truth is that typically one of the doppelgängers succeeds in their devilish desires, curing themselves of Paradox Psychosis and setting things right in the universe, an unfortunately mundane conclusion to a horrific problem.

Paradox Psychosis is an affliction we take extremely seriously here, and it's recommended that if you or any coworkers find yourselves suffering from one or more of these symptoms, it must be reported to HR immediately. It is our responsibility to rid timelines of these discrepancies before they spiral into a much larger headache.

~~You can help yourself remember it with this simple mnemonic device: Dead Investors Enliven Enterprise and Uphold Heirs. Really rolls off the tongue.~~

Not going to help anyone.

ANALYSTS

If Special Ops are butchers, whacking away and praying for the best, then ~~Analysts are wizards, creating magic from nothing~~. Each decision they make is carefully planned to the last millisecond to ensure minimal damage to the timeline. Take Herb for example, an outstanding Analyst who has tackled some of our world's most mind-bending dilemmas. A local celebrity around here, Herb is kind and principled, one of the few Analysts who is brave enough to stand up to the Handler. His greatest talent is his perseverance. It's been rumored that he once went through twenty-seven cans of Diet Coke while concocting the Lincoln assassination and all that needed to be done was giving John Wilkes Booth's barber food poisoning. One bowl cut later, Lincoln was done for, and Herb had pulled off a strategic masterclass.

Cut the hyperbole

Hyperbole!

What makes this job so hard is that Analysts must provide color to the unknown. Whereas Special Ops are tasked with solving problems they can see, a clever Analyst must foresee problems that are ultimately hidden from them. There are actually two approaches to solving anomalies, which has caused a divide among Analysts. The first approach is to be expected: mathematics, logic, and critical thinking. Analysts from this school of thought frequently spend weeks on a case, concocting a flawless fix. Their chalk usage is rivaled by none. They will fill dozens of blackboards, putting together the perfect solution for every anomaly. The enjoyment comes in this meticulous approach. Herb was once quoted as saying, "Logical reasoning is the most fun you can have with your clothes on."

Then there's the second line of thinking, a small-but-vocal coalition of Analysts that use a much different method. We'll call this group our

Generous

To say the least

"free thinkers." This subsection of Analysts will usually take a highly active psychedelic, let their brain run rampant for forty-five minutes, and then claim they've arrived at a spotless solution. As you can imagine, these solves are highly hit-or-miss. And if I must deride Special Ops for their profligacy, I'd be a hypocrite if I didn't condemn this self-indulgence and holier-than-thou thinking. Even so, some of the greatest solves we have ever had have come during these doors closed, lights out, transcendental experiments. My point is that there is more than one way to skin a cat, and we need to roll with the punches and accept alternative ways of thinking in order to get the job done. We work alongside infinity every day, so we should never limit ourselves.

The ideal candidate for an Analyst position must be able to disconnect themselves morally from their own thought process. They must have the ability to think critically while also being fluid and adapting to the problem at hand, as it will probably be a moving target. They must be comfortable working long hours in less-than-ideal conditions and be willing to join the current Analysts on their weekly lunch outing, a Tuesday afternoon trip to the Commission deli (these can drag on for upward of seven hours). Lastly, an Analyst must be satisfied knowing that they aren't the star of the show and will always be an unheralded member of any Commission team.

How They Do What They Do

Changing time (and yes, bottoms up if you've made this a drinking game) is extremely difficult. There are no perfect fixes when you're talking about something as complex as altering a timeline. Not only do ripples happen, they're so common that we've learned to plan for them. ~~Again, our goal isn't to avoid the splash as we dive headfirst into the pool but to reduce its size.~~

Cut, this isn't a poetry reading!

This means every cog in our machine must work together seamlessly. It starts with an Analyst crunching the numbers and finding the perfect approach to take. Then a plan is sent out to agents in their mission prep, and then, of course, we rely on the ever-unreliable agents to bring us across the finish line. It's an imperfect process, but it's what we have to work with.

Feels sarcastic

Our process may seem extremely arbitrary, but it is a tough undertaking that is not for the faint of heart. Analysts create a flowchart

"Where there is a will, there's a way."

Successful plans: **17**
Longest shift: **36 hrs.**
Typewriters used: **56**
Coffee preference: **Mocha**
High school clique: **Nerd**
Favorite movie: *Inception*

ATTRIBUTES
- Intellectual
- Cunning
- Prognosticator
- Obsessive

GOALS
- Foresee the future
- Limit splinters in timeline
- Get home before 10 P.M.

BIO
Monique is a caffeine-addicted night owl that's known for staying at the office late and working even harder. Her claim to fame is designing the chess game that led to the Louisiana Purchase. She's famously tough on typewriters as she types at about 150 words per minute and the machines struggle to keep up. Monique is an example of a committed Analyst that doesn't let things like mental health and her physical well-being get in the way of doing a good job.

FRUSTRATIONS
- Lack of time
- Lack of pay
- Lack of respect

TECHNOLOGY
- Blackboards
- Typewriters

PERSONALITY

INTROVERT		EXTROVERT
INTUITIVE		SENSING
THINKING		FEELING
JUDGING		PERCEIVING

for each event and then model out different approaches to solving the overall issue. Then they track the ripples each change will make, and so on and so forth. Here's where the analogy of the splash in the pool rears its ugly head. Even if a path is successful in achieving the intended goal, Analysts need to make sure that any offshoots of the plan do not lead to any larger deviations.

But why? What is all this critical thinking and protocol meant to achieve? Events in the timeline are supposed to occur in certain, very specific ways. When everything is functioning correctly, events will not deviate from what we call the "proper" timeline. Now, what's the best way to determine that a timeline is off course? For those of us at the Commission, the answer is massive cultural moments—small deviations may not register as an anomaly and can be harmless in many instances. It's when we start missing these landmark events that we know we need to step in. That's the crux of the Analysts' plight. They analyze broken timelines and deduce the best way to trigger these important events to get things back on course.

Well put!

I know some of this may seem a bit abstract and tough to conceptualize. To that I say, if you struggle with that, you may not fit in here, and secondly, I say OK, fine, let me walk you through it. Five, who I'll repeat is a legend around here, concocted the plan for the *Hindenburg* explosion in just his first day on a Commission desk. It was a miraculous coup, one that even left experienced Analysts impressed. But how did he do it? I'll show you. Here's the flowchart Five used to calculate event probability and determine how to go about triggering this event in the safest way possible.

Ha!

Don't make them feel better about themselves

Your bias is showing, but I'm intrigued.

Hindenburg Explosion

Now that we have a practical example to look at, let's break it down together. To begin, Analyst protocol dictates that three choices should be examined at a time. This is to reduce the time wasted on finding a solution. Each chain reaction will have its own ripples, and so on and so forth; by limiting the immediate actions we build from, we save time while moving toward the final result.

Could do more if they weren't so lazy…

Next, we see three branches that Five had to track and anticipate the outcomes of, following each path to its natural end in order to identify any possible hiccups to his plan. Essentially, the question is:

FIG. 2 *HINDENBURG* EXPLOSION—FIVE'S FLOWCHART

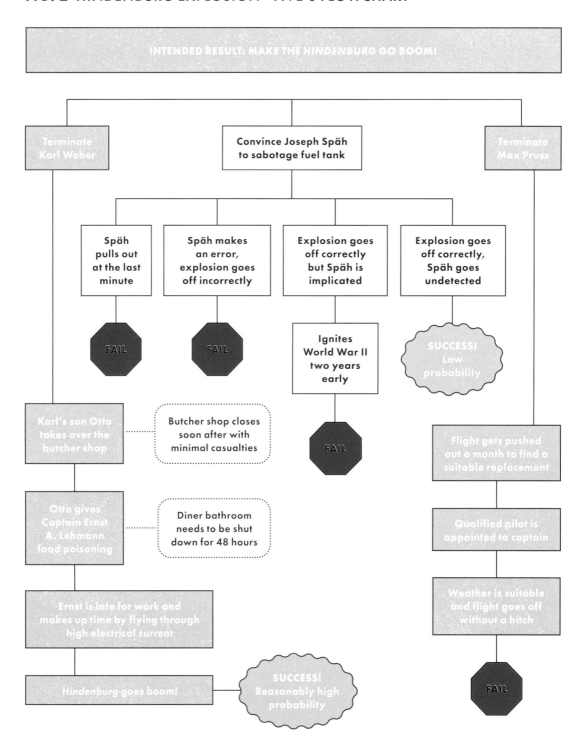

Does this pathway lead to success or failure? When your main goal is changing a timeline, the beginner searches for things that can go right, while a pro looks for things that can go wrong—a much-more-likely scenario. Then, even if a path is successful, it must be determined how likely that outcome was, and how much its splinter paths will affect the timeline. Only when an option is (A) highly likely and (B) minimally destructive is it considered suitable to be put into action.

Let's focus on splinter paths, as they determine a massive role in determining a solution's legitimacy. Some splinter paths are harmless, entertaining forays into the unknown. Imagine a situation like this: If I accidentally feed you peanut butter instead of almond butter, it may seem like a minor mistake, but if you're allergic to peanut butter, suddenly the problem becomes much graver. So when examining splinter paths, we must look behind the obvious, supposedly harmless outcomes and see if there are any underlying problems.

The path Five ended with, which is notated with a green color, features splinter paths that are essentially harmless. The prospect of a bathroom being shut down for two whole days will not affect the world in a massive way. People will tend to go on with their days since they wouldn't be visiting a butcher to use the restroom. A situation makes this path preferable, especially when compared with other possible routes.

In the second scenario, there are many splinter paths, some disastrous. For example, if Joseph Späh does go through with sabotaging the *Hindenburg* but survives and is implicated, it leads to World War II kicking off two years early, with America and Germany taking center stage in the war. It's a massive deviation from the proper timeline and thus would be a massive headache. By using these charts we can weed out paths that would create more harm than good. By following these simple methods we can help determine the correct path and save lives prior to arriving in the field.

Lincoln Assassination

This one is one of my favorites, not only because it's Herb that concocted it, but because of how it can serve as a tool for future Analysts. There's a seemingly unending desire from new blood to attack problems head-on. This direct thinking lands the newbies in some hot water. Look at the example on the following page. Working to eliminate

Not a universal truth if you have IBS ...

FIG. 3 LINCOLN ASSASSINATION—HERB'S FLOWCHART

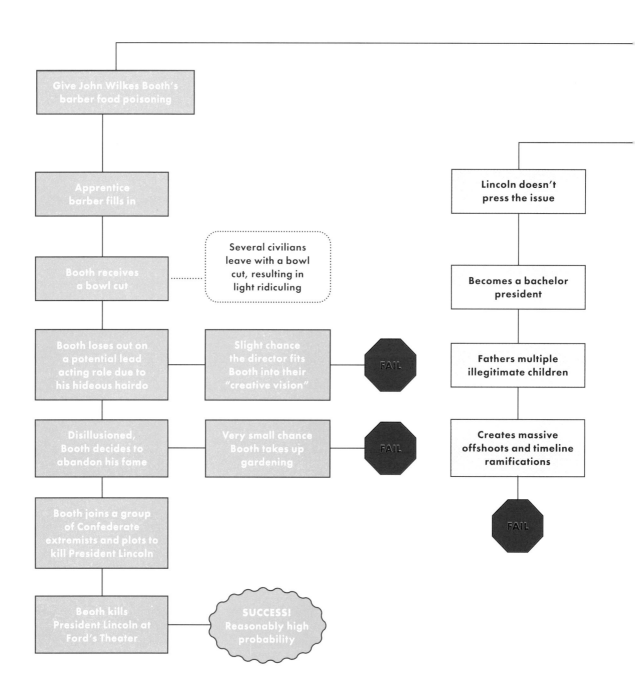

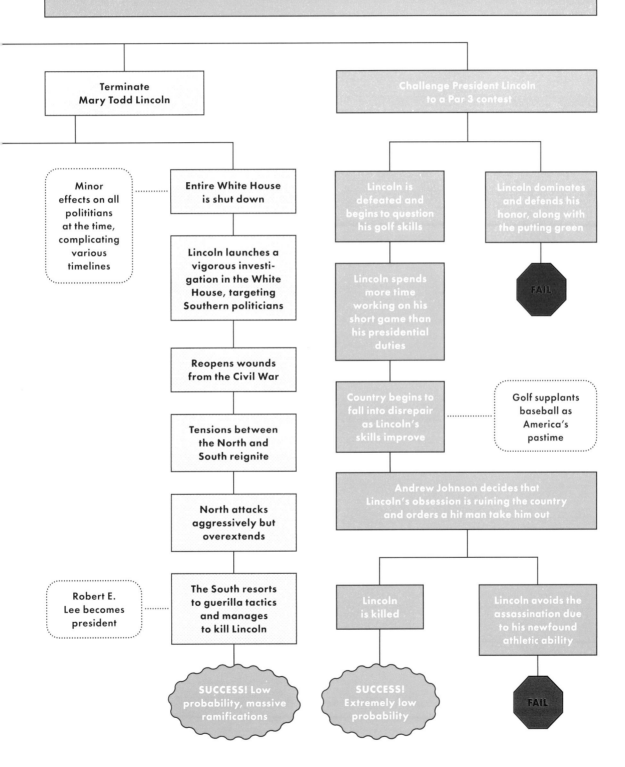

INTENDED RESULT: PRESIDENT LINCOLN DIES IN A SHOCKING AND PUBLIC FASHION.

Terminate Mary Todd Lincoln

Challenge President Lincoln to a Par 3 contest

Minor effects on all politicians at the time, complicating various timelines

Entire White House is shut down

Lincoln launches a vigorous investigation in the White House, targeting Southern politicians

Reopens wounds from the Civil War

Tensions between the North and South reignite

North attacks aggressively but overextends

Robert E. Lee becomes president

The South resorts to guerilla tactics and manages to kill Lincoln

SUCCESS! Low probability, massive ramifications

Lincoln is defeated and begins to question his golf skills

Lincoln dominates and defends his honor, along with the putting green

FAIL

Lincoln spends more time working on his short game than his presidential duties

Country begins to fall into disrepair as Lincoln's skills improve

Golf supplants baseball as America's pastime

Andrew Johnson decides that Lincoln's obsession is ruining the country and orders a hit man take him out

Lincoln is killed

Lincoln avoids the assassination due to his newfound athletic ability

SUCCESS! Extremely low probability

FAIL

Lincoln while going right at him is a fool's errand. Attempts to destabilize him may only lead to the destabilization of those around him. This is something that is absolutely important to keep in mind. When trying to affect the lives of high-ranking and influential people, it's best to try to set up your plans around their perimeter. Going at them head-on will likely always lead to far-reaching and hard-to-contain splinters.

So how does Herb get it done? He targets a flaw in the potential killer and then exploits the insecurity. He goes after a part of an actor's body that's rarely discussed but can have an outsize impact: the haircut. It's a genius move, really, subtle enough to not raise any suspicion but large enough to crater Booth's acting reputation. Additionally, targeting John Wilkes Booth's appearance also causes him to withdraw from society, meaning there's a reduction in the amount of people affected by collateral damage. From there it's set-and-forget-it for Herb, as Booth's insecurities take care of the rest. It's worth noting that it did take a while for Herb to find this solution, as we will show as we continue to examine the flowchart. There were other options that had presented themselves to him at first. The first was a pretty brutal one: terminating Mary Todd Lincoln. It's something we have to do constantly at the Commission, separate ourselves from our work. We make the hard choices here, and we do so to keep the maximum number of people possible safe. Luckily for Herb's conscience on this one, this path typically leads to failure and has a very high probability of creating undesired headaches. Additionally, by attacking someone so close to Lincoln, the path risks that Lincoln will become personally involved before the intended outcome is reached. In this scenario it's impossible to avoid, whether it's Lincoln wrongfully accusing a member of Congress or taking matters into his own hands. It pulls us away from our intended outcome while also causing a myriad of headaches. Easily something we want to avoid.

Which brings us to the third path, which look, I wouldn't be surprised if Herb did this tongue-in-cheek. Sometimes you need to have a little fun and Herb achieves that by creating a hypothetical situation where a Special Ops agent challenges a sitting president to a Par 3 contest. It's rather innocuous, but it does confront our intended subject directly. With all that said, it almost works and does actually have a reasonable probability to end in a place that we'd deem a success.

Waste of Commission resources.

Do you ever tire of waxing poetic about the pen?

Remove this paragraph. We must not breed a new generation of pacifist Analysts.

Nothing to write home about, but it has more likelihood than the more brutal option two.

~~Another lesson: Brute force is not always the right answer. As much as we love going in guns blazing and shooting to kill, sometimes a little adeptness is needed to reach our desired outcomes. This is a nod to the small group of Analysts that I had highlighted earlier, those who base their science on feeling. Their solutions tend to not include violence and remind us of a helpful tip: Reach for the pen before the sword.~~

The Moon Landing

See, it isn't all doom and gloom for us. Even when we explored the most violent and aggressive path, it led to failure. This is why we must be flexible and think outside the box.

Let's start, as always, with the solution that took the cake. It was a miraculous find by Dot, an exemplar of creative solutions to challenging problems like this. By separating Armstrong's third-grade teacher and his wife, she puts him on a path not just to love science but to obsess over it. This indoctrination at a young age is what was necessary to make sure he beat Aldrin out that door. I like the idea that her plan didn't involve a trick or any physical harm. It simply encourages the American exceptionalism that we've grown so accustomed to. Billy Masterson loses his wife, and instead of moaning about it, he throws himself into his work and inspires the next generation. This creates a motivated Armstrong, who, wary of suffering the same fate as his childhood teacher, makes space his muse in order to impress his wife. One failed marriage leads to a successful one that helps us achieve our solution. Mhmmm, I love the taste of irony in the morning.

Not how I deal with heartbreak!

Now on to the failures. Let's start with the third path because the second is too depressing to jump right into. It begins with a little old-fashioned trickery. It really is quite clever, and it's a shame this option didn't win out. The idea of breaking through NASA's security protocols to stash a candy bar in someone's quarters is bonkers. Frankly, it's enough to get your blood pumping. The problem here is the one that typically occurs in these sorts of "hands-off" paths. It leaves too many variables. Once the bar is planted, there is nothing stopping Armstrong from getting his grubby hands on it. Or even worse, we risk sending ants to space, which could have a whole separate

FIG. 4 THE MOON LANDING—DOT'S FLOWCHART

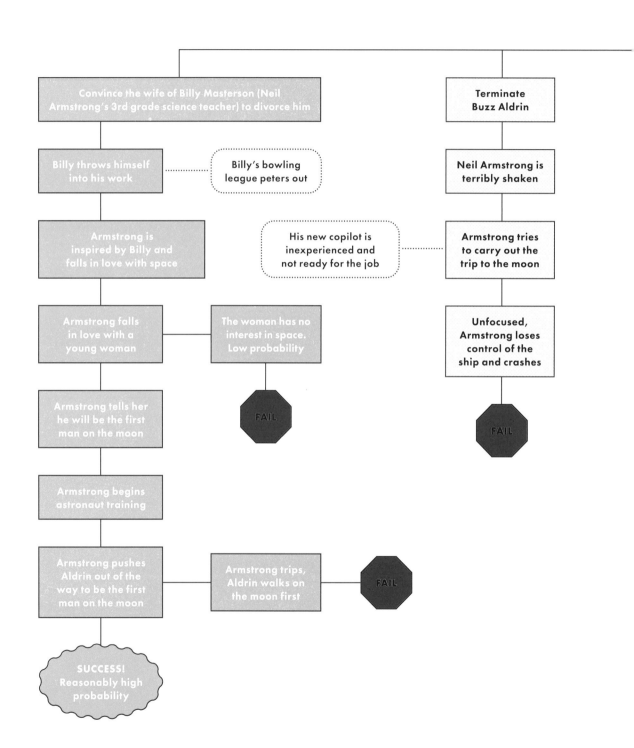

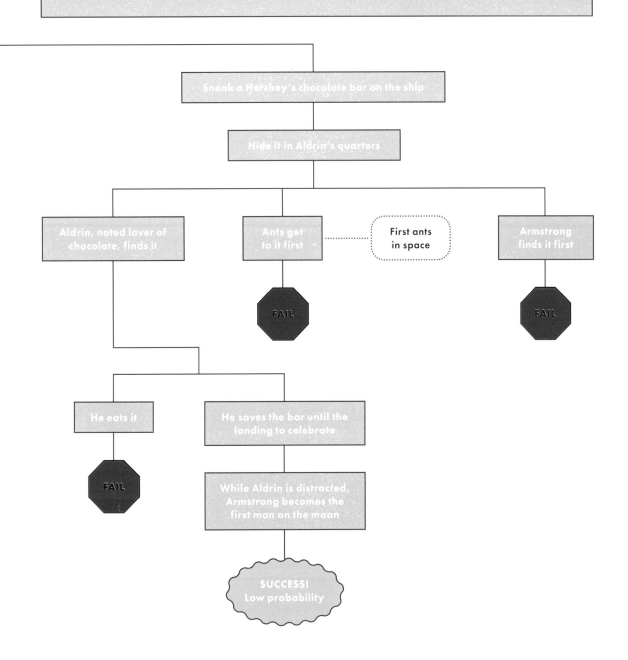

INTENDED RESULT: ENSURE NEIL ARMSTRONG IS THE FIRST MAN ON THE MOON.

Sneak a Hershey's chocolate bar on the ship

Hide it in Aldrin's quarters

Aldrin, noted lover of chocolate, finds it

Ants get to it first

First ants in space

Armstrong finds it first

FAIL

FAIL

He eats it

He saves the bar until the landing to celebrate

FAIL

While Aldrin is distracted, Armstrong becomes the first man on the moon

SUCCESS!
Low probability

set of problems. I mean, have you read *Ender's Game?* We want to avoid situations that we can't guide along the way, ones that rely on dumb luck to come through; we simply couldn't risk Aldrin being the first one off that ship, even if we had to achieve it with a little less flair.

Look, there's no way of getting around this, Option number two is extremely morbid. It's the sad reality of the field we work in. When deducing a solution, it's always going to be top of mind to off the person that's in direct conflict with what you want. It's worth noting that there are a small percentage of scenarios where this would actually constitute the proper solution, but typically beginning with such a dramatic kickoff will only lead to various headaches along the way. This is what I want to stress, and if you learn nothing else from me during this book, please remember this: the past is a fickle thing, we may find it easy to take big swings and prioritize grand gestures when trying to morph it to our will. Our job is to work within the constraints of time, <u>not to bend it to our will</u>. *Says who?*

Now that you're here, it may seem easy to lay the world's problems at the Commission's feet. I mean, don't we control everything? Wrong, so wrong. If that's your point of view at this juncture in the book, I haven't been doing my job. The Commission's mission statement is one of noninterference. Keep in mind a successful mission is one that does not lead to further repercussions. That's why everything we do is so high stakes. One mistake for us can trigger a massive splinter in the timeline, something we never want to do purposefully.

An event we're always rumored to have had involvement with is Stonehenge, very likely aliens. I mean, no humans on earth can lift stones that high, right? It's impossible to achieve. . . . I'm being sarcastic. You force enough people to work for you for free and you'd be surprised how much you can achieve. I'm looking at you, pyramids. The human race can be needlessly cruel when left to their own devices, so much so that they'd rather blame an extraterrestrial life-form than themselves. I digress.

One thing we did have involvement in? Watergate. Yeah, Nixon was up to some pretty wild stuff. Dude was a maniac and couldn't be left in charge.

INFINITE SWITCHBOARD OPERATOR

Many recruits are turned off by the Infinite Switchboard, considering it to be outdated and too complex. They couldn't be more wrong. The briefcase may transport you through time physically, but the switchboard puts you in the position of an omniscient god. But like everything here at the Commission, my job is to let you know how it works, so let's dive into it.

In the previous section, I mentioned that when timelines diverge from massive cultural events, it is brought to our attention as an anomaly. That's where the Operator comes in. They are hawks staring down infinite timelines in infinite eras looking for any imperfection. So yes, the switchboard does give them the ability to be an <u>all-seeing being</u>, but they may also be training in the history of the world in order to know when an event is not occurring properly.

Intentional rhyme?

The training our operators undergo is meticulous. They are expected to know every single event in human history. In order to retain this knowledge, they are given pop quizzes at a brutal rate of <u>thirty to forty</u> times a day. Lucky recruits are also given old tapes of *Jeopardy!* to watch, as it's been approved as an official resource by the Board.

Oh please, it's twenty-five at most!

The Operators at the Commission are a collection of oddballs. There aren't many of them, and their position requires them to work extremely long hours, so they don't have much of a social life. Due to this, a strict requirement is a lack of social skills, thus ensuring there will be no distractions on the job.

The ideal candidate can adjust to multiple situations at a moment's notice. They must be experts at prioritizing a single issue and identifying it for the Commission. We rely on the Infinite Switchboard Operators to not only spot anomalies when triggered, but to determine the time period and make a quick decision on what exactly is going on and how it should be dealt with.

"Your friendly eye in the sky."

Anomalies located: **147**
Hours logged: **24,563**
Debates resolved: **84**
Vitamin D level: **Low**
High school clique:
Gleek
Favorite movie:
About Time

ATTRIBUTES
- Quick
- Assured
- Decisive
- Good eyesight

GOALS
- Watch the switchboard
- Spot anomalies
- Don't get caught looking at anything weird

FRUSTRATIONS
- The urge to watch weird stuff
- Small screens
- Uncomfortable chairs

TECHNOLOGY
- Infinite Switchboard

BIO
Glenn is as committed a worker as you will find, typically logging eighteen-hour days. He had his mother sew a cushion for him to use while sitting in his chair to help reduce the strain on his back. Glenn enjoys sneaking people into the Infinite Switchboard room and resolving debates by zooming in on any moment in question. Since Glenn typically doesn't spend much time outside, he enjoys looking at images of open fields when he comes across them on the Infinite Switchboard.

PERSONALITY

INTROVERT				EXTROVERT
INTUITIVE				SENSING
THINKING				FEELING
JUDGING				PERCEIVING

Infinite Switchboard

The Infinite Switchboard is kind of like the universe's coolest cable package. On its screens, you can see every event that's ever occurred. In a way, that's the downside—you really *can* see everything that's ever happened, which is incredibly difficult to sift through.

That's why the switchboard was designed to track anomalies, which are considered statistically significant breaks in the timeline. They're most often caused by members of the Umbrella or Sparrow Academies due to their immense and unique powers, but there have been massive moments independent of the academies that the switchboard has caught. I'm sure you've heard about the saying "that every time a butterfly flaps its wings, the future changes," blah, blah, blah. Well, that saying is a bunch of bologna. A butterfly flapping its wings has never hit the Infinite Switchboard's radar, and why would it? A little flap here or there has no effect on the surrounding world and barely has one on the butterfly itself.

Especially Viktor and Five

It's important to filter out the noise and diagnose major problems immediately. That's what the Infinite Switchboard does and what makes it so important.

The Tubes

The tubes; let's talk about 'em. One of the main questions recruits have is how it works, so let's dive into it. The answer may surprise you. Think of any point in a timeline as an open vent in a ventilation system; the tubes function as central air. The Commission's reach is overwhelmingly large. We're proud to provide service into every single home on Earth, and for that we have the tireless, oft-unheralded workers on our construction team to thank.

The process—smooth and almost always ending in a successfully received message—wasn't always like this. At one point, messages were carried by ravens, who were forced to deliver messages into disastrous situations. As

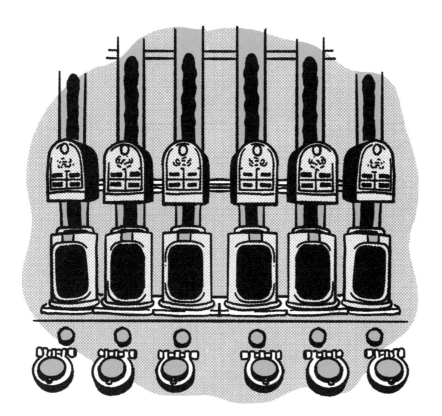

you could imagine, <u>results varied.</u> Later, our system evolved into something akin to Morse code, but slightly different. Instead of a spaced-out rhythmic and easy to translate code, it was more of a knee-slapping sound. It was up to agents to determine what the slaps meant. Do two slaps mean terminate, or do three? Valid questions, as the answers were different depending on what orientation team you had been siloed into.

Many good birds were lost in those days.

Unfortunately, when our company promoted synergy and the constant changing of teams, disastrous results occurred. Although we publicly deny our involvement with the Mongolian invasions, let's just say that if a few messages were a little bit clearer, there would have been much happier villagers in Eastern Asia in the thirteenth century. In short, these were the early days of the Commission when regulations were minimal and poor judgment was rampant. We lost great agents back then due to poor communication. Now the issue is that agents willingly disobey direct orders. I guess things truly never improve. You have to love the humanity of it all.

delete

It's remarkable that we've improved so much since those days. Today's system works by using modern infrastructure as a delivery mechanism. When messages are sent through the tubes, they are transported to their specifically designated location and time. They then are incorporated into whatever pipe system is most readily available. Allowing the messages to be retrieved in phone booths, medicine cabinets, or even vending machines. If a place in the timeline has any connection to interior infrastructure, whether it be sewage or electricity, tube messages will find their way there. So while the efficiency of our current tech may be mind-blowing and tough to believe, just know that it did not come easily.

HR

At a company as large as ours, the HR department can tend to be a bit discreet. They prefer to conduct their work in the shadows, passing down edicts without the slightest bit of input from employees. I suppose it may be for the best. We employ countless trained killers, so it tracks that we'd want to keep the people restricting their parking spots anonymous.

Not much is known about how newbies actually find their way into the HR department, but I've heard a few theories. The main one is quite sad: Essentially, those sent to HR are the absolute rejects, the runts of the runts of the runts of the litter. The people we were told were sent packing and granted generous severance packages could actually be the ones silently controlling our work life. This seems like the simplest answer to me, and it makes sense that the scorned rejects would take their anger out on those they find undeserving.

Auggie, of course our HR department exists, they are located off-site to limit negative interactions with our workers.

The other main theory is that there isn't any HR department at all. The facts support this theory. They have no wing in our headquarters, no number to call. They send messages out, but there's no way to contact them. Thus allowing the Board to have full control of a typically wayward aspect of a company.

My opinion on an ideal candidate? Have no real technical skills and pride yourself on your ability to talk to people, even though in actuality you make everyone you come across extremely uncomfortable.

PROFILE: HR – TALIA HIGGINS

"Not our problem."

Work avoided: **Infinite**
Problems caused: **4,313**
Arguments resolved: **0**
Chair: **Reclined**
High school clique: **Popular**
Favorite movie: **Up**

ATTRIBUTES
- Lame
- Lazy
- Chatty
- Machiavellian

GOALS
- Find ways to cut money from employees
- Prop up legacies
- Head home after lunch

FRUSTRATIONS
- Doing their job
- Giving raises
- Letting someone else talk

TECHNOLOGY
- Instagram
- Twitter

BIO
Talia spends a lot of time working from home; in fact, there's little data to show she actually comes into the office at all. She spends most of her time scrolling through Instagram or Twitter trying to follow the latest trends. I suppose Talia does find time to seek out potential new recruits every now and then, but that claim is difficult to substantiate. Talia, if you happen to read a draft of this before it goes to print, feel free to let me know what you've accomplished here.

PERSONALITY

INTROVERT	·······························X·	EXTROVERT
INTUITIVE	·····························X·	SENSING
THINKING	····························X·	FEELING
JUDGING	X··························	PERCEIVING

The Candies

Our HR department utilizes an odd candy in order to understand different experiences across timelines. They fly a bit under the radar for most of our new initiates, despite the fact that they are one of the most miraculous inventions we have here. It stands out not for its usefulness, but because it's simple and proves our overwhelming ingenuity. If you don't know what I'm talking about, I feel sorry for you. Our HR department has managed to concoct a piece of candy that is flavored unconventionally, not cherry or chocolate or vanilla, but rather, it's flavored like any era in the history of the timeline.

And I know what you're thinking: that's asinine, impossible, and simply not true. And to that I'd say I did agree with you once. I too thought it was nonsense, crafted by worthless sommeliers sitting around a chimney fire saying things like, "It does have an oaky scent, doesn't it?" But I was wrong. My first bite was North America in the year 1776 and it was . . . triumphant. I thought it was a fluke, a stroke of luck. And then I dug into Rome in the year 117, and it was everything, wide-ranging, powerful, emotional. In those moments, you realize how you reduce your environment to only a few ways of tasting. Spicy vs. dull.

My favorite candy to munch on is Chicago in 1985. I mean, who can forget the Mike Ditka-led Bears team and that defense?? There was U2 and Blondie, music still on MTV.... I digress.

Sweet vs. dry. It's an oversimplification to the umpteenth degree. We take this endless world and try to stuff it in a duffel bag in an attempt to make sense of our surroundings.

I had many different candies that first day, and I won't expand on the harsher ones. 2020 USA is particularly rough. But what I take from that time is that even as we try our hardest to preserve this world and keep it pure, evil can still find a way to seep through the cracks and infect a time and place so cruelly that it can be tasted for an eternity later, whether we believe that to be possible or not.

IN MEMORIAM

As expected, time is an impossible thing to quantify at the Commission. We have the ability to travel through time and revert the past almost anywhere, but we are not all-powerful. What I mean to say is that despite our ability to jump from timeline to timeline, we cannot revert time here at the Commission. That means those who die here truly die for good.

Five has what can be described as a unique relationship with the Commission. At times he has been a great ally to us, in other moments he's been a great adversary. Five can be quite ruthless and is responsible for the deaths of multiple influential members of the Commission. Prior to their deaths I had been working on sections for these members, but after their passing I've updated them slightly. As a new member, it is beneficial to give you a sense of those who have come before us so we can learn how to move on without them.

Pretty tame way to say murderer.

"Leave no trace."

Successful missions: **367**
Success rate: **94%**
Civilian casualties: **1,421**
Conscience: **Muddled**
High school clique: **Artist**
Favorite movie: *CHIPS*

ATTRIBUTES

- Confident
- Dangerous
- A little scary
- Killer bond

GOALS

- Find Five
- Torment civilians
- Look sick

FRUSTRATIONS

- Agnes (for Cha-Cha)
- Briefcase maintenance
- Seeing out their masks

TECHNOLOGY

- Quirky helmets
- Unlimited weaponry

BIO

Hazel and Cha-Cha were two of our most storied agents. Their prowess is well respected in Commission lore, and they were typically sent out on missions deemed too dangerous for their coworkers. They had a bit of bloodlust and were known to rack up higher body counts than necessary on their missions. Their helmets were some of our finest tech, able to deflect bullets as well as other larger impacts.

DECEASED

PERSONALITY

INTROVERT	⋯⋯⋯⋯⋯⋯⋯⋯⋯⋯⋯⋯⋯⋯⋯⋈⋯⋯	EXTROVERT
INTUITIVE	⋯⋯⋯⋯⋯⋯⋯⋯⋯⋯⋯⋯⋈⋯⋯⋯⋯	SENSING
THINKING	⋯⋯⋯⋯⋯⋯⋯⋯⋯⋯⋯⋯⋈⋯⋯⋯⋯	FEELING
JUDGING	⋯⋯⋯⋯⋯⋯⋯⋯⋈⋯⋯⋯⋯⋯⋯⋯⋯	PERCEIVING

Hazel and Cha-Cha

Hazel and Cha-Cha were two agents that represented the old guard of the Commission through and through. They were brutal in battle, racking up obscene death counts on every mission they were sent on. So what went wrong? <u>Hazel went "soft"</u> (gained a conscience) and the duo crumbled like a month-old graham cracker. You see, Cha-Cha took kill-at-any-cost to extreme measures, and when Hazel wouldn't follow suit, the pair turned on each other. Suddenly, their directive was no longer to kill Five but rather to kill each other. Needless to say, it was <u>an HR nightmare.</u> This incessant infighting is exactly what I would like to avoid in our next generation of recruits. You have a partner in the field for a reason: you watch their back and they watch yours. It's how this whole thing is supposed to work. When you're worried about the knife they wield being lodged in your back instead of someone else's, the whole system falls apart.

hey!

You're right about that.

The Swedes

The Swedes are, without a doubt, the most famous trio the Commission has produced. The brothers formed their bond at an early age while hurting squirrels and were marked as natural fits for Special Ops. Oscar, the youngest brother, died in a trap that was originally laid by the Handler. Otto, the middle brother, died at Axel's hand as Allison used her powers to control the eldest brother. ~~Axel exacted his revenge on the Handler and then left the Commission.~~ While his location is currently unknown, he is heavily suspected to have joined Klaus Hargreeves cult, "Destiny's Children."

Delete, unsubstantiated.

"Öga för öga."

Successful missions: **75**
Success rate: **89%**
Civilian casualties: **21**
Conscience: **Silent**
High school clique: **Geeks**
Favorite movie: *Rent*

ATTRIBUTES
- Quiet
- Tight-knit
- Revenge-driven
- Blond

GOALS
- End the Umbrella Academy
- Use Duolingo
- Wear cute clothes

FRUSTRATIONS
- The Handler
- Allison's powers
- Rising trench coat prices

TECHNOLOGY
- Blond hair dye
- Coordinating outfits

BIO
Ahh, the Swedes, a mercurial trio of brothers. They were no-nonsense killers who would only attack civilians if they could confirm they had contact with one of their targets. They were cold-blooded and willing to do anything to defend each other. While it has been argued that their hair was all-natural, I believe that L'Oréal blond hair dye is the only product that could achieve such a color. While they didn't wear matching outfits, they did always try to coalesce around an aesthetic, lest anyone forget that they were not only brothers but a powerful unit as well.

PERSONALITY

INTROVERT	⋈························	EXTROVERT
INTUITIVE	····⋈·················	SENSING
THINKING	···········⋈·········	FEELING
JUDGING	·············⋈·······	PERCEIVING

DECEASED (MOSTLY)

Gloria

Maintain a safe distance from Five.

You may wonder what Gloria achieved to deserve her own section, but the more practical question may be, <u>what *didn't* she do?</u> Let me explain.

Gloria was the final piece in a long line of telephone. She was responsible for sending messages through our sophisticated tube relay to our in-field agents. It's a job that may seem simple in retrospect— it was anything but. You see, Gloria was responsible for properly communicating *every single thing* we did here. One incorrect message had the potential to send a timeline into a complete tailspin. ~~Now, without her, we're struggling to keep things operating smoothly.~~ *Delete, no need to include that.*

And one of the most taxing on our yearly budget.

In order to keep up her routine, intense focus was needed. Gloria was well known for having <u>one of the toughest morning routines in the universe.</u> This schedule should give a good sense of how grueling her days were:

2:30 A.M. — Wake up

2:45 A.M. — Meditation

3:15 A.M. — Breakfast

3:40 A.M. — Sudoku

5:30 A.M. — Post–mental exercises meal

6 A.M. — Call Mother

7:30 A.M. — Review daily tube messages

8:30 A.M. — Cryochamber recovery

9 A.M. — Snack

10 A.M. — Send out tube messages

1 P.M. — Lunch

2 P.M. — Send feedback to Analysts for unapproved messages

3 P.M. — Swim one mile

3:30 P.M. — Snack

4 P.M. — Mental exercises No. 2

5:30 P.M. — Socialize with coworkers to learn their innermost desires

6 P.M. — Dinner

7:30 P.M. — Bedtime

Understatement

This may seem a bit excessive. And it may also seem like <u>she spent way too much time eating or playing Sudoku than doing her actual job.</u> But that's not the point. It was all about preparation for her, and being in the correct mental state. Gloria was undoubtedly the best at what she did, and since she's been gone we've all struggled to fill her shoes. There was no one else like her; that's why we put up with the nonsensical schedule.

PROFILE: GLORIA

"Often imitated, never duplicated."

DECEASED

Messages sent: **92,345,678**
Puzzles completed: **532,489**
Snacks devoured: **134,432**
Enlightened: **Was**
High school clique: **Teacher**
Favorite movie: **N/A**

ATTRIBUTES
- Gloria
- Gloria
- Gloria
- One of a kind

GOALS
- Properly communciate messages
- Snack
- Complete 10-plus mental exercises

FRUSTRATIONS
- None

TECHNOLOGY
- Tubes

BIO
An absolute tour de force and the former be-all and end-all of the Commission. Those who have had the blessing of being in her presence revel in the experience. She's truly the only one who was capable of pulling off her job and ensuring all communication is seamless. It's hard to imagine the Commission will carry on without her.

PERSONALITY

INTROVERT ··X EXTROVERT

INTUITIVE X·· SENSING

THINKING ····················X························ FEELING

JUDGING ································X········ PERCEIVING

The Board

No way to speak about the deceased.

The Board was an odd collection of folks who <u>clawed their way to the top of the corporate ladder</u>. While they would like to think they were a mystery to us worker bees, it was well known that they would meet at a specific time and timeline every three months. Now I know what you're thinking: *That really narrows it down.* And you'd be right; this should be more than enough to keep things on the down low. ~~Unfortunately, the only mid-level member of the Commission they inform is the Handler, and, well, she told Five. Like they say in England, the rest was bloody history.~~

Delete, no one needs to know this.

No one is quite sure what the Board actually did. Similar to Corporate America, it's unclear if their job description included anything other than wearing designer suits and siphoning egregious sums of money from our paychecks. With that said, they were the ones responsible for calling the shots even when it wasn't exactly clear what those shots were.

Enough slander.

AJ Carmichael

AJ Carmichael was the most recent Chief of the Commission. He was also a Shubunkin goldfish with the ability to pilot a robotic body. You'll see a lot of strange things in your time at the Commission no matter what department you end up in, but you'd be hard-pressed to find one stranger than AJ. A question I assume you'd like to ask is how his whole . . . what should I call it? Situation, worked. The fact is, I don't know. Nobody does except for AJ, and sadly, <u>the secret died with him.</u>

Is it not obvious?

AJ was definitely a capable leader, but unfortunately his lack of coordination meant he couldn't outrun an ax-wielding Five. I do wonder if the commission could have found a return to form under AJ's leadership. Alas, we will never know.

"Let them eat cake."

Record score: **63**
Preferred club: **Driver**
Decisions made: **7**
Brunch order: **Mimosa**
High school clique: **Rich kid**
Favorite movie: **Babylon**

ATTRIBUTES
- Golf
- Brunch
- Infinity pools
- Multiple homes

GOALS
- Avoid the office
- Stay under par
- Charge it to the company card

FRUSTRATIONS
- Work
- A sense of self worth
- The question, "What is it that you do here?"

TECHNOLOGY
- Raya
- Vanguard

BIO
Percival could typically be found hitting the links and putting for par. When he wasn't kicking some brews back at the country club with the guys, he was managing his investments and deciding where he would go for vacation that week. It was never a dull moment with Percival as his Raya account was typically being blown up at all hours from matches across different times periods. It's rumored that he once took Cleopatra out on a date. I asked him for confirmation but he said he didn't kiss and tell.

PERSONALITY

INTROVERT		EXTROVERT
INTUITIVE		SENSING
THINKING		FEELING
JUDGING		PERCEIVING

DECEASED

"Don't push me over."

Bodies utilized: **23**
Mile time: **6:43**
People fired: **5,483,959**
Favorite fish food: **Tetra**
High school clique: **Principal**
Favorite movie: **Jaws**

ATTRIBUTES

- Swimmer
- Leader
- Scientific marvel
- Well-dressed

GOALS

- Keep his head on straight
- Get his mile time down
- Swim often

FRUSTRATIONS

- Logic
- Using the restroom
- Missing the ocean

TECHNOLOGY

- His own body
- Bass Pro Shops

BIO

AJ was the king of the castle, and he came by it honestly. Frequently mocked as a recruit, AJ rose in the ranks to become the big cheese. He was smart, well-intentioned, and brutal in battle. He was an experienced agent who returned to the desk life. His intentions were the same as mine: keep this place running smoothly for as long as possible.

PERSONALITY

INTROVERT	EXTROVERT
INTUITIVE	SENSING
THINKING	FEELING
JUDGING	PERCEIVING

DON'T LOSE TRACK OF TIME!

DEVIATIONS WILL **NOT** BE TOLERATED

COMPANY CULTURE

Auggie, just write the darn book.

Unnecessary; may I remind you this is an employee handbook.

What I fear is typically lost in these types of sections is honesty. How can I comment on company culture when I am fundamentally a part of it? Instead of telling you about my journey here, I'd like to show you. I'm attaching an excerpt from my personal diary in the hopes that by sharing my experiences, I may enrich someone else's.

Day 17

Tomorrow is the day I am finally called up to the big leagues. After seventeen days and sixteen evenings being shuttled from orientation to orientation and watching training videos on repeat, I have been deemed worthy of ascension.

In my quiet moments, I wonder what happened to the students that could not keep their eyes open throughout the training. One day they were beside me in class, underachieving, the next day they were gone. Rumor around here is that they were handed a generous severance package; one that ensured we wouldn't hear from them again. I'll let you do the math there.

But not me. I've been bumped up immediately. I always knew I was special. I was meant for this, but now it was clearly confirmed by the people I admired so deeply. One more thing in my favor, I've been assigned to one of the most powerful people at the company, the Handler. With her effervescent flair, she's hard to miss, and why would you want to? She is a symbol of empowerment that the Commission could provide me. All I need to do now is learn.

<u>I'm going to be happy, fulfilled, and hopeful for my future.</u> :)

Oh my. I didn't know you had an optimistic side.

Day 18

If I had a briefcase, I would travel back to yesterday and smack myself in the face for my unwarranted positivity. I would not use the word "mean" to describe the Handler, because mean is a word we use to describe human beings, and she is anything but.

My morning began with a giant red flag being waved in my face. I was called to the Handler's quarters, where I found a note that told me to wake her with an a cappella rendition of "She'll Be Coming Round the Mountain When She Comes." She does not wake lightly, as a bronze statue of a lion was chucked at my head. Had I not been quick to dive out of the way, I'd have a hole in my head the size of Death Valley.

Next, it was time to help her get dressed, which may sound like an easy task but is anything but. She has so many clothes that I had to be sent to several different rooms to grab a bow tie or brassiere. These things were not easy to find, as each was piled high with clothes; so high that I legitimately considered finding an earring the equivalent of a backpacking trip. I disassociated with my body soon after, so I can't recall much until dinner, when the Handler had me cook her favorite meal, Kraft Mac and Cheese that has the pasta shaped like SpongeBob SquarePants characters. While I was shocked at the order, it seemed to calm her down quite a bit, and I was able to slip out of the room as she fell into a food coma. I decided to add these memories to my diary as quickly as I could, as I fear the full day will be repressed imminently.

Objectively hilarious

Day 25

I'm sorry I haven't added to you in quite some time, but I have been preoccupied with my assignment. I check in with other assistants as I pass them in the hallway, and I'm horrified by the gap between our experiences. One student got to travel with a briefcase, another was even allowed to use the Infinite Switchboard for a moment. How could I be so unlucky? I figure a past version of myself had done something to deserve this.

I write this today because the Handler and I have just had our one-week check in. It began in her office with the stench of her oddly shaped pipe filling the room. After my prolonged coughing fit, which she defined as "pure evidence that I would never make anything of myself," she informed me of my current progress. I showed no aptitude for Special Ops, and she was completely disappointed in me. And while I wanted to correct her and tell her that of course I showed no aptitude, because I was meant to

shocking

be behind a desk saving lives instead of in the field destroying them, I didn't have a chance. There wasn't time for me to get a word in edgewise between her ceaseless talking and interspersed, uncontrollable coughing fits. No matter; despite her negative words, it's been determined that I continue "learning" from her for the next two weeks. I cannot think of a greater punishment.

After discussing with a friend, I believe it would be unwise to fill these pages with my whining, depressing as my life may be at the moment. There is more to life than hating your boss and stressing over their insecurities.

Future Auggie, you may forget the above words, but I hope you remember them when you flip through these pages. Also, I had chicken tenders at the cafeteria today. They were solid.

I'll end my diary excerpts there; unsurprisingly, it got worse because of course it did. The Handler's abuse continued. I received a swirly and was sent back to the Stone Age to retrieve a rare gem for her. After being impaled by a saber-toothed tiger, she considered me graduated. I was reassigned and another poor lackey took my place. I do not wish my experience upon anyone reading this book. But it _is_ my experience.

Throughout this book I will be honest. I have said that before but let me reiterate my promise. There is too much at stake here for you to enter the Commission uninformed.

Need less of your personal insight.
This should read neutral, and professional

ACCOMMODATIONS & ATTIRE

No need to dissuade them of that thought.

People expect the Commission facility to be a place of splendor. A wide-open emporium of never-ending wealth devoid of negativity. But just like everyone else, we at the Commission are penny-pinchers, and the best place to save money is the same as it's always been: on the youth. Trainees are unpaid until formally initiated into the Commission. This means that all your time watching videos, practicing techniques, heck, even reading this book, is unpaid. This is to encourage more effort from our newcomers in the hopes of someday attaining a career that will pay them in more than just experience.

Delete

~~Upon admission into the academy, entrants are asked to put two hundred dollars down to pay for their attire at the school. An additional two thousand is used to pay for their meal plans, a standard two meals a day plan at our cafeteria.~~

Then there are the dorms—built with brick and sculpted by the gods—for our beloved inductees, because sleep is a known benefit in the development of our youth. In truth, our quarters leave much to be desired. Once you enter through the creaky front door, you will be greeted by drab gray walls adorned with peeling paint and assorted holes created by enraged former students. You better hope your room is on the first floor, because if not, you will need to brave the creaky wooden stairwell that hasn't been repaired since, well . . . no one quite remembers.

Things don't improve much when you enter the rooms. The scent of moldy mattresses pounds you in the face as you come through the door. If that isn't enough sensory overload for you, your roommate's

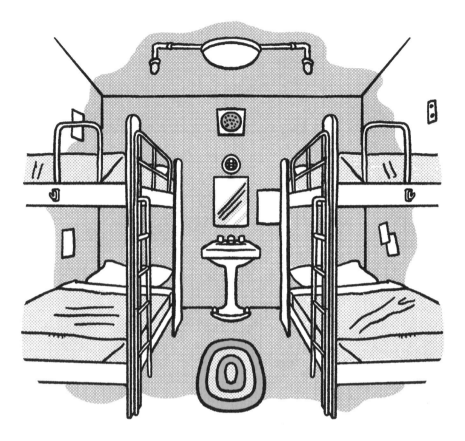

bed will be about five feet from yours. Better hope they have good hygiene! <u>You share a bathroom and three showers with more than thirty other people your age,</u> and one of the sinks will somehow never work. Oh, also, you're on your own for the first time in your life and your hormones are raging. Good luck getting a good education.

    Each floor has a dedicated break room where trainees can take part in leisure activities, like playing *Pong* on an old TV or playing board games with friends. The space is meant to bring you back to a simpler time where you didn't always know what everyone around you was thinking; a time where debates were settled with confidence and loud screaming, not on the internet. A time when frankly things were better, right? You see, the people on the Board at the Commission were very insistent that those below them spend their free time honoring the time period they grew up in. Which is predominantly the fifties if that isn't clear. They want to strand you in their thinking and proclaim that they know best. It's their reward for educating the new class, gaining a

The joys of youth.

Rolling my eyes at this.

new army of followers who can tell their story. And they may be right, because history is written by the victors, and then maintained by the educators.

Attire is strictly professional. The majority of our employees wear two-piece suits in order to give off the impression that we have a handle on what's going on here. Female employees are allowed to wear skirts that can be no shorter than four inches above the knee. We consider ourselves extremely progressive. Despite all the rules, there are plenty of exceptions made for attire if they add to something to an employee's aesthetic and help them look, and I quote company policy here, "rad."

Students are required to return their suits to their closets at the end of each day. The suit is then replaced with a near duplicate by the next morning—although some have murmured that it's the same suit

SINGLE-
BREASTED

SUIT TO BE
WELL-TAILORED

SUIT TO BE
WELL-TAILORED

TIE MANDATORY

BLACK OR DARK
COLORS ONLY

SKIRT FALLS JUST
ABOVE KNEE

SHOES POLISHED

SHOES TO BE MODEST
AND COMFORTABLE

coming back the next day uncleaned. The charade does a nice job of convincing trainees that their money was well spent . . . without any proof of results. Trainees are also fined for alterations to their uniform. That means no spills of any kind, especially of the blood variety. Special Ops agents who are meant to kill can't even get a little bit messy without incurring extra charges. ~~Sounds like a scam to me.~~ And don't even think about adding mustard and relish on your hot dog at the deli in fear that it explodes on your uniform.

Delete.

FOOD

Cafeteria food is simple and non-offensive. Different departments are allotted separate meal plans. Special Ops are given a carb-heavy diet as their travel tends to lead to . . . well, let's call it an upset stomach. We've narrowed time travel down to a science, but there are surely still kinks to work out. A common dish for Special Ops is buttered pasta with a side of steamed broccoli. Special Ops are known for dousing their meals in hot sauce "in an attempt to feel something," yet it is rarely enough to sustain them. Due to their lackluster diet, it's estimated that Special Ops eat upward of five meals a day while on assignment in order to expand their taste palates on the company dime.

Thank you for bringing this to my attention.

Analysts are given a hard-core diet of veggies and energy drinks. When projects push them to stay up at all hours, they need to be able to keep up. Black coffee is on tap 24/7 as well. Analysts are not permitted to add any additional sugar or spice to their diets, as their mind must be focused solely on their jobs, not exploring new flavors. With that said, they are permitted to go trick-or-treating on the Commission grounds every Halloween, and they then try to maintain that stash throughout the whole year. *A lot of interesting insight in this section...*

The Handler doesn't eat in the dining area; meals are crafted for her and brought to her office to her specifications. At least, that's what she thinks. One of the first Commission secrets I learned when working for the Handler was that she is actually served food from the common cafeteria. The only difference is that it is presented in a way that feels high class and exclusive. A meager hamburger can become a vaunted filet mignon if you're too busy and consumed with how one of your 347 hats looks.

No office is free from political warfare, and the Commission is no exception. The most aggressive war zone is the fridge. That's right, we have one fridge. Now don't get me wrong, it is quite large, at a healthy 31.6 cubic feet.

The Handler takes up a large portion of it, and it's worth noting that other higher-ups have never been spotted either putting something into the fridge or pulling something out. This leads us to believe they have their own off-site break room, where they are free from the rabble of the masses. The microwave is another battleground. There are some ground rules that most will find universal. We always cover our sauces, and we never, ever cook fish if we can help it. Nothing from past the year 2050 is allowed to be put in the microwave as well, since the buildup of microplastics in the food makes it liable to go *boom*. I know these rules may seem frivolous, but when you're sharing an office with so many people who are literally trained killers, a little common courtesy may save your life.

Way to bring the energy in the room down.

DON'T TAKE A
WRONG STEP

ALWAYS
CHECK YOUR BRIEFCASE!

DEPARTMENT FUNDING

The ones who sign
your checks?

There's a joke around the Commission that goes, "When we're not downsizing, watch out for pig droppings from the sky." You see, we always seem to be in a recession, cutting back on pay for travel, cutting down on desk space, cutting down on, well, anything the higher-ups can get their greedy little hands on. It has hit everywhere. When the Commission started, Special Ops teams were sent out in groups of five, specifically put together to make sure each member complemented the others in full. These squads were insanely efficient, playboy agents were weeded out, and true leaders found themselves in charge. But unfortunately, they still weren't successful no matter their preparation or conviction. Despite having every advantage, they failed more often than they succeeded, and it wasn't very close. So it was decided that cuts would be made, because if we're unsatisfied with the department's performance, why not cut resources?

Always a lower-level
employee annoyed at
the sensible decisions.

The Commission's failures became a self-fulfilling prophecy; we'd prohibit our agents from getting the help they needed while admonishing them for coming up short in impossible situations. Soon the Special Ops teams shrunk as well, going down to four and then three until we reached today, where most teams travel in pairs of two unless it is otherwise necessary to remain in groups of three. I'm looking at you, Swedes.

Did anyone
think they were?

If you think the Analysts were saved in all of the cutbacks, you'd be terribly wrong. It's true that Analysts are typically low-maintenance worker bees, but that doesn't mean they wouldn't enjoy the comforts of middle-management office life. Each Analyst used to have their own office, complete with a desk, chair, and even a blackboard to scribble out their flowcharts. Yet it's been a free-for-all when it comes to pulling back funding for the lifeblood of the Commission. Soon private offices became shared, and now Analysts are left in small classrooms together, about twenty-five apiece. Crammed in like sardines and given only typewriters to solve the biggest problems in the timeline. You'd think the Board would protect the time and thinking space of their golden geese, but they've specifically gone out of their way to make the lives of their most valuable employees harder.

The break rooms have taken the hardest hit. They used to be a rarified paradise, replete with shuffleboard and a punch bowl deeper than the Mariana Trench. There were even plans for a Ping-Pong table to be added and, let me tell you, the people were psyched. There would have been a true tournament, Special Ops vs. Analysts. Gloria vs the Handler. It would have been a true coming together; the synergy I always dreamed about, but alas, the plan was scrapped after yet another year of negative revenue.

This actually does sound fun.

WEAPONRY AND THE BATTLEFIELD

Here's the good stuff

I know I can come off as a bit of a kvetcher in this book, and that feedback would be fair. I advocate for the truth at all times, and I don't blame myself that it can very often lead to me being an adversary of the Commission. But when the guys upstairs get it right, it would be wrong of me to not give them their due. What's fair is fair, and <u>as far as weapons are concerned, the Commission truly gives its field agents carte blanche.</u> There are the standard-issue Glock 9s, sure, but beyond that is the opportunity to be creative. Some agents choose to carry mini-guns or use sniper rifles (with no scope just to prove their worth). Everything is personally designed. From my studies, the oddest weapon in the field was a tambourine that had the jingles honed to a sharpened edge. The coolest, of course, were double katanas. Despite my goal to one day man a desk, I do appreciate the Commission's leniency in this respect. I mean, seriously, these people are putting their lives on the line and deserve, at the very least, to go out knowing they fulfilled their creative potential.

What would I select if I were in the field? <u>I'm glad you asked.</u> It's a no-brainer that tracks back through my ancestral line to the twelfth century. My ancestors wielded a great mace that held the moniker "Doom Breaker." It's slightly unwieldy, weighing <u>more than sixty-five pounds,</u> but when it connected, it was absolutely game over. Now, I'm sure you may be hesitant to believe that I can swing a weapon like that, but I'll have you know I take Pilates classes three times a week, so I'm not worried about it.

What weapons do Analysts use? The pen is the Analyst's analog for their sword, and they wield it with intent to kill. There's been some talk that by limiting the technology available to Analysts, the Board is merely saving on costs, but in this respect I disagree. Flat-screen TVs and large monitors do nothing but slow down the pace of work in the office, that much is inarguable. How is someone supposed to track the

No one did.

Auggie, you can't lift that

Finally, a section where you get it. Love the note on personalization. This will entice recruits into the business, especially Special Ops. I know you didn't ask, but I will share my ideal weapon with you as well. When I was young, my father... sorry, I'm rambling. It would be a flamethrower. I must admit, you have sent my mind racing. Good work!

effects of getting a cat neutered when there is online shopping to do? By keeping the tech nailed down in the past, Analysts are encouraged to use their own minds (the most powerful weapon of all) to crack cases open instead of relying on antiquated AI or data processing.

You can find most of the famed Commission weapons in the above rendering of AJ's old office. But as a special treat, I'd like to share with you three weapons that are legendary around here because of how they broke the mold. Fasten that tie of yours, because this is going to be a bumpy ride.

THE PREPOSTEROUSLY POISONOUS RUBBER DUCKY

This mouthful to say was wielded by the storied Commission agent Juniper P. Constantine. Juniper had a very colorful aura. She was always smiling and was constantly carrying a sunflower in her front pocket. In short, Juniper was a master of disguise.

I know I mentioned earlier that agents weren't always sent into the field to kill, but not all agents were like Juniper. She was immaculate, proudly repping a 99.3 percent success rate on over 600 attempts. *Impressive!* Her plan was simple: She'd use her fun, no-frills persona to gain entry into a target's home. Once inside, she would excuse herself to the restroom and drop one of these duckies into their bathtub. With only one exception, the target would see the ducky and remark at how strange it was. But then, spurred on by Juniper's creative energy, they would come to their fatal conclusion, "Wouldn't it be fun to take a bath with a rubber ducky?"

Once exposed to warm water, the ducky would release a poisonous venom into the water that would seep into the pores of the unwitting victims. Targets would only survive about three minutes before falling under, but at least they got to go in an ultimate state of relaxation.

TWINS WITH TEN-FOOT NUNCHUCKS

A complete waste of resources.

This weapon is not known for its effectiveness, (I mean that much should be clear by the illustration) but rather by its novelty. Identical twins Veronica and Viola Winters were brought to the Commission due to their unorthodox fighting style. The pair would wield a pair of nunchucks between them and use them to confuse and combat their enemies. Well, that is when they worked, at least.

You see, a pair of nunchucks is an extremely difficult weapon to wield on your own but are almost impossible to use alongside a partner. But the Commission kept sending these two out on missions because they never complained and always tried their best.

Ultimately, more deaths were caused by people accidently crashing their cars while trying to get a look at this bizarre scene, and the two were forced into retirement. Reports have stated that they do appear as sidewalk performers on the Vegas Strip from time to time.

JUST A PAPER CLIP

This weapon is known for its simplicity, wielded by none other than the famed assassin Niko "Nighthawk" Oliveria. Niko enjoyed the freedom that came with his gig, and performed his duties with an air of class. Niko chose to use a paper clip instead of a standard-issue pistol because he believed it separated him from his colleagues.

Niko would work slowly, needing to amass over one thousand pokes with his paper clip to create a wound large enough for an infection to form. This meant that he would sometimes spend years trying to take down one target. Some saw it as a waste of resources, but most saw it as a thrilling showcase of determination.

Unfortunately, Niko couldn't keep up his game for long, and he was killed by retaliatory gunfire while trying to prick what he thought to be an unsuspecting victim. I guess what they say about bringing paper clips to gunfights proved itself to be true that day.

Gone too soon

What a heart - throb he was…

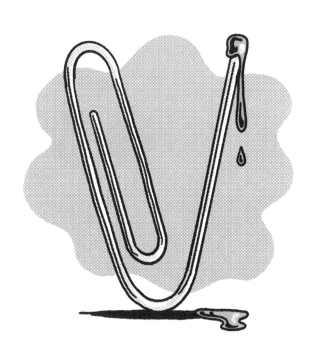

VACATION TIME

The Commission is an on-call 24/7 job. You get into this business because you want to change the world, not because you like to take midday siestas. That's not to say people don't get creative to find time off. There are fights between Special Ops to get assigned to easy missions in beautiful locales. One time, an agent spent two years on assignment in Tahiti, citing an intelligent adversary that was keeping him from completing his task. His task was to steal a candy bar from a local shop, and it turned out that his adversary was a playful German shepherd that the owner kept in the shop as protection.

It's trickier as an Analyst who is bound to their desk much more strictly. There are work-arounds, though, and Analysts can apply for a tourism permit that allows them to travel to any time period they would like in order to conduct research. This research is then shown to a panel of their peers and can be used to obtain a grant. These research grants are extremely difficult to get, and the findings are kept under lock and key, leading many to believe that it's all a big ruse put together by the higher-ups so they can hoard all the vacation time for themselves.

You have brought a lot of interesting info to my attention. Thank you, Auggie.

FROM THE OFFICE OF THE FOUNDER

Auggie, reading your thoughts on the Commission and
our cutbacks has made me feel empty inside. It is
true, when we began we were truly ambitious, a power
to be reckoned with, but we just kept losing. I
didn't want to pull back at all, but as the Founder,
I don't answer to myself. I answer to a Board that
was invested in us either winning or mitigating our
losses in the event that we failed. If it were up
to me, we'd increase our presence thirtyfold, but
there just aren't enough resources available to us
to accomplish that. We exist in an odd space, don't
we? We're almost independent from the rules of time
itself, but no one, even us, is completely free.
It could be said that we're all stuck in our own
prisons, and all briefcases do is change the view...

I have been somber lately; my health is fading, and
it's forced me to really examine the choices I have
made. I want so badly for this experiment to work,
but as I approach the point where every breath will
be a battle, I'm forced to consider if all of this
energy, pain, and suffering is worth it. I'd like to
think so, but currently the prognosis doesn't look
great.

But you have my promise. As long as I breathe, I will
keep fighting.

A **MESSY** DESK
IS A **MESSY** FUTURE

KEEP YOUR DESK
CLEAN

UMBRELLA
ACADEMY
DOSSIER

UMBRELLA ACADEMY (+ LILA)

It's impossible to write a book about the Commission without also writing about the Umbrella and Sparrow Academies. These are people who, while kind at heart, end up being our nemeses more often than not. Their powers make them massive threats to the timeline; essentially, each one is an anomaly in and of themselves. They are nuisances across all timelines and never fail to give us a hassle.

In this section, we will break down each of them: what they're like, and the best ways to combat them. While they exist across most timelines, it would not make sense to speak about them in general terms. To simplify things, I will discuss what I'll refer to as their "Alpha" forms, the ones that are currently giving the Commission so much trouble and meddling with our activities. I will list the siblings not in numerical order like their adoptive father, but rather in order of how often they typically distort timelines. I will also discuss an item that _No need to include!_ should be included in each briefcase in order to best combat them. Additionally, I will highlight the most common lives they lead in alternate timelines in order for you to always be prepared in the field.

VIKTOR HARGREEVES

Viktor Hargreeves is the one Umbrella Academy member that consistently causes the most destruction to timelines, surprisingly higher even than Five. He was born in Saint Petersburg, Russia, to a mother who participated in aerobic gymnastics. As a young child, Viktor's powers were suppressed by his adoptive father, Reginald Hargreeves. This caused him to not develop full use of his powers until later in life, which makes them extremely tough to control.

Viktor is what we like to call a kamikaze. He has such a tremendous impact on the world, including himself, that the destruction he can cause can be massive and hard to logically comprehend. You see, there are many people with outsize influence—presidents, billionaires, etc.—but within these people there's a self-awareness and understanding that their decisions and actions can drastically disrupt the course of reality. But with Viktor, decisions tend to be made impulsively and emotionally, meaning they're extremely difficult to predict and even harder to contain.

Viktor's talent has always been about his immense ability to manipulate the world around him. He can take the beautiful symphony of an orchestra and turn it into a weapon. In distressed situations, Viktor has been said to enter a dispassionate state, where his eyes and body turn white. Viktor's powers can be unpredictable and unstable, and that's only heightened in intense moments. This means that his impact on the world around him exponentially increases at times when he does not intend it to.

Viktor has been known to be able to launch shock waves that expand out from him and forcefully propel assailants several feet backward. This can make Viktor difficult for agents to approach, meaning you should always try to attack Viktor from behind if possible, as a fair fight is <u>nearly impossible</u> to come by. On a cooler note, Viktor has been documented as having the ability to levitate off the ground, which is why each briefcase is fitted with a mini extendo-ladder to help agents get to hard-to-reach places. That's a joke—one that isn't funny, but a joke nonetheless.

Viktor is truly one of the rare people the Commission struggles to combat. Even with all of <u>our wacky tech, protocol, and wit, we're still no match</u> for the walking neutrino bomb that is Viktor. He is a

Don't frame him as an unstoppable force.

making us sound weak

reminder of our place in this universe, and I will apologize for repeating myself. We exist to maintain the balance, not create our own. If any Commission member could harness Viktor's power, I have no doubt this universe would be ripped apart at the seams, so let's all thank our lucky stars we have never recruited Viktor to the Commission.

Combat Tactics

For missions concerning Viktor, briefcases should be equipped with a cyanide pill that will induce death upon consumption. It's a much more palatable death than accepting your fate at his hands. *Not funny*

Alternate Timeline

You can most commonly find Viktor teaching violin at an underfunded elementary school in Saint Petersburg. Viktor knows the kids struggle to afford their instruments, so he works at a coffee shop on the weekends and uses the extra money to help ensure each kid has something to play. Viktor uses his abilities to harness sound in order to amplify their music in spite of the underdeveloped auditorium they play in.

FIVE

By all accounts, <u>Five is a legend around here.</u> He's worked in Special Ops, he's worked behind a desk, he's done it all. He's the only known human that's learned how to travel through time without the aid of the Commission. He has completed a record 767 missions despite being in the Commission's employ for a fraction of his rivals' time. He's taken down some of the strongest assassins in modern history with the ease of peeling a banana. Hell, he's taken out Commission employees. And he's done it all with his signature style and flair. Five uses his genius intellect more often than his physical prowess in order to always keep opponents on edge.

Five is a rare case because he will fight either for or against the Commission, depending on which option will benefit his family. This makes him easy to predict as long as you can understand what is causing him distress.

Despite his small stature, Five is a natural-born killer who's been sent to complete some of the Commission's most harrowing missions. He is calm under pressure and thinks with logic instead of emotions. He is ruthless in battle and will show no mercy to anyone that threatens him. It is well noted that the best way to deal with Five is through fervent discussion. If you can make something sound logically appealing to him, there's a good chance he will go along with it.

Five's main ability is referred to as "blinking." With this power, Five can jump through time and space and disappear. This makes him slippery in battle, and an absolute pain to deal with. Five's small stature is due to the fact that he's trapped in a thirteen-year-old version of his body; this makes him easy to underestimate. There are multiple reports of Commission agents fleeing the scene after a threatening encounter with Five. It is recommended that <u>all Special Ops agents remain on guard while interacting with young boys,</u> in the rare event that one of them may be Five.

Five's responsible for some of the most famous kills in the Commission's history, chief among them the assassination of President John F. Kennedy. Five is the only field agent with a perfect kill record. No other agent has been so successful in the field. He was recruited to the Commission by the Handler; unsurprisingly, the most impressive feat she has achieved in her time here. Five was recruited due to his powers

Should be in prison.

I guess we never did have a good read on him.

Lost many good men that didn't pay attention to this.

and education, which made him, in the Handler's words, "the perfect killer," but she never understood what propelled him and kept him working so hard. When Five escaped the Commission and went back to save his family, the Handler was dumbfounded. I was not.

Five's ability to travel backward and forward in time is not widely reported and hotly debated. There are some at the Commission who think that traveling without a briefcase is impossible. They argue that in order for Five to travel through time, he would disrupt the laws of the universe. It's funny the miracles one can experience while still doubting the existence of others elsewhere. *groan*

Others (the rational ones) have formed a general consensus that while Five has the ability to travel through time, it's unpredictable and unstable. While it can achieve the same effect as a briefcase, it's nowhere near as safe. We know this because of Five's fervent search for a briefcase when he loses possession of his own.

Good point!

The most important thing about Five is that he serves as a window into what the Umbrella Academy kids are thinking. Despite all of Five's achievements—master assassin, cold-blooded genius, time traveler—he is above all a pragmatist, and is always willing to avoid conflict when possible. While many Umbrella Academy members are quick to anger and violence, it's Five who can be trusted to take a deep breath and make the correct call.

Combat Tactics

For Five, every briefcase should be fitted with a pair of handcuffs, since he cannot blink if his hands are restricted out of his view. *Is that verified?*

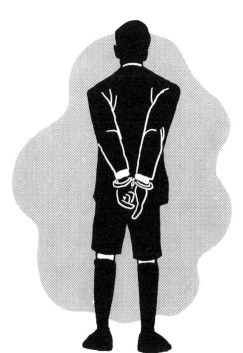

He looks a little too like the Founder in this illustration; revise

Alternate Timeline

Believe it or not, Five isn't commonly found overthrowing governments or leading revolutions. Free from his obligation to save the world, Five is most likely to be found serving a different lord as a stay-at-home dad in Dublin, Ireland. His wife, a fashion model named Delores, is known for her hauntingly simple and statuesque poses.

FROM THE OFFICE OF THE FOUNDER

The way you write about this boy... or man, I'm not
quite sure. It reminds me of someone I've lost.
It's hard to admit this, but what I do can be time-
consuming, pun intended. I'd like to spend more time
reflecting on who I was before all of this. If I'm
being honest, I don't remember my own name, it's been
too long. Now I'm the Founder, and that's enough.
Everything else has fallen by the wayside.

Oh, what a joy it is to be young. To dive headfirst
into a problem, no matter how large, believing you
can fix it. I spend a lot of time alone here, and
until I read this book, I felt as if I had lost
touch with the thing I built. I struggle to believe
how that's possible. Do you understand that? No,
you couldn't possibly understand it. I created this
thing. It only exists because of me. Yet it lives on
without my daily input. I have made something that I
don't have the power to control. Do you understand
how terrifying that is?

I think about the first time Five traveled through
time. There he was, just a child, blessed with a
power that was spellbinding. But when he used it,
he was lost. Stranded in an apocalypse nowhere near
his family. What I mean to say is this: Unimaginable
power is attainable, but harnessing that power in a
way that works as intended every single time...

Well, that may be impossible.

ALLISON HARGREEVES

Allison continues to be one of the hardest Umbrella Academy members to predict. Her power can be ruthless and unstoppable without prior training. By saying, "I heard a rumor," Allison can force an enemy combatant to do anything her heart desires. For example, if Allison says, "I heard a rumor you punched yourself in the face," you're going to be in for a headache. I've even heard that Allison no longer needs to say the "I heard a rumor" preamble, which makes her even more terrifying.

Hearsay.

What separates Allison from the rest of her siblings is her ability to manipulate the universe to her will. Luther can pick up heavy things and put them down. Allison, on the other hand, can convince a man to abandon everything he knows and kill his own brother. They're playing on completely different levels of power. But don't worry, there are ways to keep the upper hand. There is considerable data to suggest that Allison often abandons her powers due to their outsize effect on the world. In this state, Allison is extremely weak and easy to deal with. But be wary. When threatened, Allison is quick to abandon her supposed morals, which is why you should always be prepared to slit her vocal cords as a precaution.

Yes, we need to drive home the moments where we can mentally defeat these people.

Allison is a massive adversary to our mission. We want to set things right, keep them proper; she wants to bend the universe to her will.

Allison is consistently protective of her daughter, Claire, and has earned herself the nickname of "Momma Bear" around the office. Protecting her daughter makes Allison not only more likely to use her powers, but additionally more likely to use them on a grand scale; so much so that they will literally bend the universe. It is therefore advisable that all agents strictly stay as far away from Claire as physically possible so as not to throw the timeline in irreparable flux.

Combat Tactics

For Allison, a pair of noise-canceling headphones should be included in every briefcase to limit her powers. I'm confident that trading your ability to hear in order to keep your free will is a balanced one.

Would this work?

Alternate Timeline

Allison is most likely to become a politician. With her quick wit and her propensity to seek adoration, it's a natural fit. Allison typically starts out in the local scene before building to a larger national platform. Her catchphrase is, "I heard a rumor that taxes will not be raised!" Allison's biggest supporter is Claire, her mighty daughter who's always at her side.

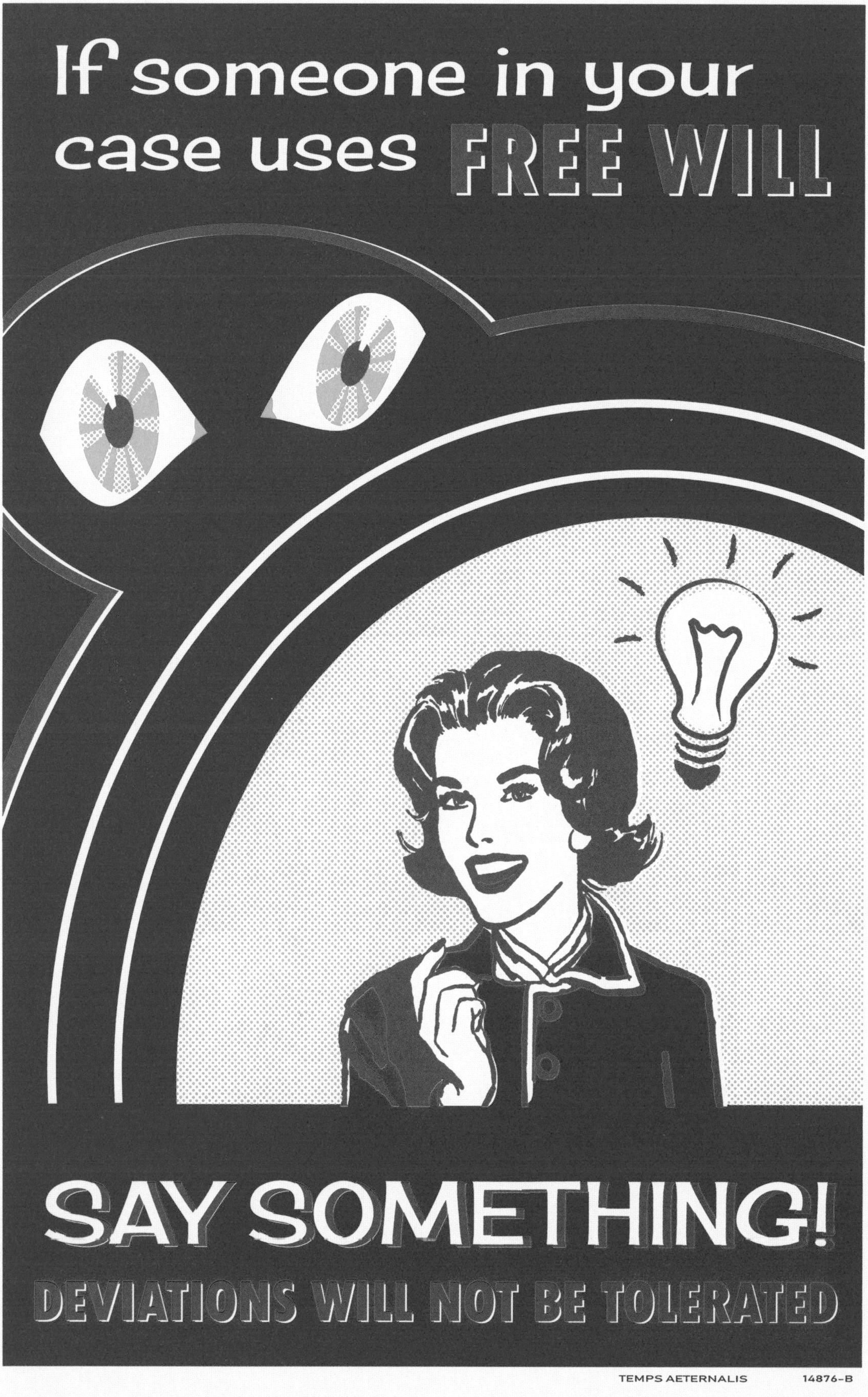
If someone in your case uses FREE WILL
SAY SOMETHING!
DEVIATIONS WILL NOT BE TOLERATED

TEMPS AETERNALIS 14876-B

KLAUS HARGREEVES

Frequently underestimated, Klaus can surprisingly be one of the most impactful members of the Umbrella Academy on the timeline. He's erratic even when sober, and his propensity to indulge in drugs and alcohol make him extremely difficult to understand, especially to himself. One time, a blacked-out Klaus led to a coup of the state government of Wyoming because a large majority proclaimed him to be a god after seeing him stumble away from a car wreck. He was installed as a religious leader for fourteen hours before the National Guard came in, and Klaus sobered up long enough to apologize for the proceedings.

That's actually quite impressive.

Klaus's place in the Umbrella team was always under scrutiny as a kid, and if it wasn't for Viktor, he would have likely found himself as the odd man out. Never the strongest fighter, Klaus always felt like an out-of-place liability in the heat of battle. Klaus would hang back with Reginald and provide a type of ground support, communicating with the dead to help plan the best route for the team. While his help was always welcomed, it certainly wasn't necessary, and his lack of responsibility led to Klaus falling behind his siblings in training. As he grew older, Klaus honed his powers by staying sober long enough to learn how to control them. Soon, not only could Klaus communicate with the dead, he could reanimate them, something he did with his brother Ben to help in battles, and also (this is rumored) let Ben sleep with a woman. A sober Klaus is right up there with his other siblings in terms of pure power. Simply bringing Ben back for a short period is more than enough to make Klaus feared, but it goes deeper than that. His connection with the dead makes him an extremely effective carrier of information, capable of knowing secrets long thought to be lost to the sands of time. In a way, his mind is a briefcase in and of itself. He can bring the past into the present by simply closing his eyes. He's remarkable.

After being reunited with a version of his father from the Sparrow timeline, Klaus mastered his ability to reanimate himself. Imagine being so hammered you never realize that you can't die. In fact, it sounds like a Special Ops agent's wet dream. Klaus managed to achieve the impossible. It was one thing to communicate with the dead, but to cross over to the other side and then return? Well, look, the discovery was timeline-breaking, and threw everything out of whack over at the Commission. Imagine that? A human playing by a completely different set of rules than those around him. These discoveries helped add fulfillment to Klaus's life, but it also made him much more powerful and landed him on our radar in a significant way.

As Klaus cannot be killed, lethal force is unnecessary with him and is considered a waste of energy. The better option is to tie him up, or better yet, restrain him in a way that he cannot control his limbs. It's funny how quickly immortality can turn from a power into an instrument for torture. ~~For the sadistic agents at the Commission, coming across Klaus can turn into quite the eventful trip.~~

Delete—I'd like to keep that secret for myself.

Combat Tactics

For Klaus, I recommend that a joint be included in every briefcase in preparation for coming across him, since all that is needed to avoid conflict with him is having a swell time. Additionally, a bag of hot Cheetos should be included as well, in the event that things really ramp up.

Sadly, this would work!

Alternate Timeline

Klaus typically finds himself growing old in an Amish community in rural Pennsylvania. The lifestyle suits him, and he uses his spare time to write poetry on parchment about the simple joys of life. His works receive national acclaim, and he leaves the community a few times a year to read his material at small fairs. Despite the positive tone of most of his writings, a few do recall voices from the grave. Klaus attributes these poems to his alter ego, "The Séance."

BEN HARGREEVES

Ben Hargreeves's personality, unsurprisingly, depends on the timeline you find him in. Umbrella Ben is kind and sweet but died at a young age in a tragic incident. Umbrella Ben has been noted to accompany Klaus due to Klaus's ability to bring forth spirits from the dead. Despite Ben's passing in the Umbrella timeline, he remains a person we absolutely need to be aware of. Ben's powers are freaky, awesome, and terrifying.

Umbrella Ben has the ability to summon a tentacle monster from another dimension through his stomach. This causes Ben a great deal of physical pain. Umbrella Ben is a pacifist who would have never seen battle if it were up to him, and would have preferred to be left in a cottage by the sea. This makes Ben extremely dangerous, as he will try to avoid conflict at all costs. ~~So if the tentacle monster enters the playing field, there is not much either you or he can do at that point.~~ My advice would be to use the briefcase to escape. In lieu of that, I'm not sure. . . . Pray?

Delete, we always have a resource. We're the Commission

Umbrella Ben is selfless in ways that can be hard to explain without fully knowing his relationship with his siblings. It is widely accepted that Ben is responsible for absorbing the blast from Viktor's breakdown that ended the Alpha Umbrella Academy members' second timeline. In the field, Special Ops agents can struggle with their capacity for empathy—doing so when confronting Ben will leave you headed in the wrong direction. He is honest and loyal to a fault and will go to great lengths to defend his family at a massive cost to himself. So please, if you encounter Ben in the field, be ready for him to do whatever it takes to defend those around him.

Combat Tactics

For Ben, I recommend that a box of Girl Scout cookies is included in every briefcase for him, to help him calm down and keep the tentacle monster at bay.

Alternate Timeline

Ben can most often be found as a high-level chef in Seoul who specializes in preparing seafood. Ben's hatred of tentacles led him to the profession, and people come from far and wide to try his famed San-nakji.

DIEGO HARGREEVES

Diego Hargreeves is a jack-of-all-trades, a vigilante with a passion for vengeance. Outside of Five, Diego is the only member of the Umbrella Academy to work for and visit the Commission. Diego managed to escape from his intro session (a dream of many young recruits) and hop on the Infinite Switchboard. Essentially, if you write the perfect first day, you'd be hard-pressed to differ much from Diego's. Even so, he couldn't evade security for long, and he was quickly apprehended. Diego's folly shows how <u>you must be on guard at all times at the Commission,</u> as outside forces may try to use our technology for their own good.

Also, quite good-looking

Great point to highlight; we're tough as nails!

Diego is a master knife thrower who can alter the flight path of projectiles with his mind. Ever the underdog, Diego takes pleasure in bringing so-called justice to those he sees as evildoers. He uses a boosted police scanner to arrive on the scene of the crime before the actual cops can get there. Despite his solitary lifestyle, he has been known to work alongside police and likes to think of himself as Batman-esque; not the savior the world wants, but the one it needs right now, yada, yada, yada. Diego is often seen practicing his knife throwing, curving them around walls to hit hard-to-reach targets. Diego uses knives instead of guns because they are "generally badass" and require intense skill. Even though Diego's powers typically manifest in controlling blades, I have it on good authority that he could control an entire battalion's worth of bullets given the right circumstances.

Understatement   Diego is <u>not a strategic fighter.</u> He can be caught going in guns (knives) blazing without fully assessing a situation. This means that traps and mind games are an effective way of deterring Diego. With that said, he has a good heart and fights with conviction. If he gains the upper hand on you, you'd have immense difficulty fending him off. Additionally, due to his vigilante background, Diego shows no feelings of kindness toward hostiles. He will kill—and kill quickly—if threatened.

Diego is caring and, despite his better judgment, will usually sacrifice himself for the benefit of his family. Diego is known to have a rivalry with Luther, as the two constantly bicker over which of them should be considered the leader of the Umbrellas. This rivalry was fostered by their adoptive father, Reginald Hargreeves, in order to create competition between the two. While they have grown closer in recent years, it is never a bad idea to create conflict between the two in order to cause a distraction and throw them off their game.

Overall, it seems that Diego's impact on the timeline is quite limited. In fact, it's usually the branches that occur after Diego kills a supposed bad guy that end up causing the real waves. In one timeline, Diego accidentally killed a sitting US senator's son at a bar, and the resulting policy decisions from that event led to another Prohibition.

Combat Tactics

For Diego, a crowbar should be included in every briefcase, since it's a large weapon that isn't thrown and therefore is not vulnerable to Diego's powers.

Alternate Timeline

Diego is most commonly found playing darts and hustling people for their money in dive bars across Mexico City. He usually sends his first two shots wide of the board before hitting pure bull's-eyes for the remainder of the game.

LUTHER HARGREEVES

Luther is the de facto leader of the Umbrella Academy, <u>despite his powers being quite tame compared to his siblings.</u> His super strength and durability pale in comparison to jumping through time and manipulating sound waves.

Another understatement

Even so, Luther was an ambitious rule follower and thus earned the moniker "Number One" from Reginald Hargreeves. Luther is known for maintaining his cool on missions and <u>always sticking to the game plan.</u> His lack of ability to think on his feet has drawn the ire of his siblings but it could be argued that he creates the framework to allow their creativity to shine. Even when he was quite young, Luther had no issue taking the lead on missions and facing hardened criminals head-on. It's undeniable that he was the emotional force that spurred the team forward at such a young age.

Lame

Luther is essentially 43 percent silverback gorilla due to an incident that occurred when he was the only active Umbrella Academy member. A procedure was performed to inject his crippled body with the DNA of a gorilla. This procedure, as crazy as it may have seemed at the time, did in fact work. The only issue was that Luther, a conventionally attractive man, would be horrifically disfigured for the rest of his life. ~~With that said, there are multiple reports from women who have come across Luther at a club that said that the change "hurt in some places and helped in others." I will let you, the reader, decode that subtext.~~

Delete, gross

Luther responds to kindness above all. He is trusting and willing to put his support behind those that he believes in. His commitment to the Academy as a child left him underdeveloped romantically, and a complicated set of circumstances with his adopted sister Allison only further muddied the water. Because of the insecurities that his celibacy has caused him, Luther can be quick to anger when confused and unsure how to handle a situation where he isn't in full control. He will resort to violence when pushed into a corner and will not be able to negotiate a cease-fire without one of his siblings stepping in.

Combat Tactics

For Luther, each briefcase should be equipped with a small wooden figurine of Reginald Hargreeves. If shown to Luther, he will melt beneath his daddy problems and be an easy target.

I mean, let's be honest, no one is afraid of this gentleman, we'd be better served including a boxing heavyweight. They'd pose more of a threat than Luther. Should it be Mike Tyson? Muhammad Ali? I'll leave it to you.

Alternate Timeline

Luther is most commonly found working as a fireman in a rural Swedish town. He's a three-time annual Mr. March on the department's calendar. In his free time, Luther enjoys going to the zoo and making silly faces at the gorillas.

LILA PITTS

And a modern-day Benedict Arnold

Lila Pitts is the Handler's adopted daughter. I thought about including her entry along with those of the Umbrella Academy but decided against including her among the infamous siblings. If pressed, I'd likely slot Lila in between Five and Allison. Lila is heavily rumored to be one of the children born in 1989, along with the Umbrella Academy and Sparrow Academy kids. If you don't know about the events of 1989, it involved forty-three women across the globe giving spontaneous birth.

It is a bit strange, isn't it?

In the Alpha timeline we've been discussing, Reginald Hargreeves, ever the weirdo, went around and adopted seven children: Luther, Diego, Allison, Klaus, Five, Ben, and Viktor, who he believed to have secret powers. He was right.

Lila is the Handler's shadow at the Commission. But she's no guard dog. During my horrid time working for the Handler, it was Lila who would come to my aid when the Handler's head was turned—she'd help me collect ceramic from shattered plates or aid me in spraying Febreze when I was sent to ameliorate a "situation" in the bathroom.

Someone has a crush

There is a pureness in Lila that fights to escape the gravity of the Handler's maniacal orbit. Lila's abilities are strange, as they require the existence of members of the Umbrella and Sparrow Academies in near proximity in order to work. On her own, Lila is a skilled and well-trained fighter. She fights in a style that may seem chaotic to her opponent, but somehow, she manages to maintain complete control. Her true power is mimicry, and she comes to life when in battle against those with powers, making her the Commission's most underrated secret weapon.

Don't tell everyone!

Even Five, a trained killer, found her to be a worthy combatant, as her ability to mimic his time jumps shocked him. Viktor, whose power is unmatched by his siblings, found himself reeling when going mano-a-mano with Lila. Lila, despite her acumen in the field, is much mightier with the pen than the sword; she prefers psychological manipulation over the physical. It's a fun challenge for her to try not to tap into her terrifying powers in order to whoop someone's behind.

Due to her abilities, Lila isn't used as a Special Ops agent but rather as the Handler's personal closer. She's sent to finish jobs that the Handler wouldn't trust to a regular agent. In doing so, Lila has become a specialized weapon that's often used for brutal jobs. It worries me, as she could bring so much good and balance to the world but is used as a glorified hit man who doesn't help mend the universe but instead bends it to the Handler's will.

My hope is that <u>people like Lila, the truly special ones,</u> work to change this world for good. At the Commission, temptation is all around us. You can sneak onto the Infinite Switchboard and watch any moment in history or sign out a briefcase and find yourself across a table from Winston Churchill. Everything is so tantalizing, incredibly close and attainable for anyone here. But the power to take all this information and still choose to be a force for good? To me, that's truly heroic.

Keep it contained, Auggie

Combat Tactics

For Lila, I'd recommend including a sushi dinner in every briefcase, as she'll always chow down and put off fighting while she munches.

Alternate Timeline

Lila can be found rehearsing with her Paramore cover band at a small studio space in East London. Lila and her band, the Mimics, like to play basement shows, where they can cut the lights and rock out until the wee hours of the night.

REGINALD HARGREEVES

It's been confirmed many times over that Reginald is an alien from another world, which means he doesn't necessarily fall under our purview. We concern ourselves primarily with humans, and someone like Reginald represents an obscene anomaly. It's hard to think of him as being in the same ballpark as his adoptive children. Even so, Reginald is an extremely important person to be aware of.

Chiefly, he's the creator and de facto head of both the Umbrella and Sparrow Academies. This means Hargreeves is single-handedly responsible for bringing the Commission's most powerful adversaries to fruition. So why did Reginald do it? We have a few theories on our end. A popular one is that he'd like to reset his timeline in order to bring his dead wife back to life. In this scenario, Reginald actually acts as the Commission's direct antagonist. He intends to reset the universe that we're trying so desperately to keep running smoothly. Another theory is that he watched too much true-crime late-night TV and felt he needed to raise a family of superpowered bodyguards to protect him. The debate rages on to this day.

Reginald is a tough critic and a hard father to please. His mistreatment of the Umbrella Academy kids from a young age is well documented. His arrogance and lack of leadership led to multiple failings for his team: Luther's lack of self-confidence. Diego's lack of discipline. Allison's lack of humility. Klaus's inability to harness his reincarnation ability. Five's forty-year disappearance. Even, perhaps, the reason why Ben met an early grave. And let's not even get into the emotional abuse he hammered Viktor with during his most sensitive years.

It's funny, isn't it? How Hargreeves's failure in every aspect of his life has led to his rise and fueled the volatility of the Umbrella and Sparrow children.

His selfishness has put every potential timeline at risk. Say what you will about any member of the Commission (I sure have), but even when we fail, there's no doubt that we are the best at what we do. With Reginald, we're left to wonder, *is he particularly good at anything? Is he charming? Cunning? Or did he just get lucky?*

You will see a lot of people during your time at the Commission—powerful people, weak people, those who have been deemed negligent, the whole gambit—but it's important to remember how arbitrary the

Did you have a complicated relationship with your father? I couldn't tell after reading this.

universe can be; the fact that people like Reginald can slip through the cracks, amass millions, create empires off the backs of others, will never go away.

The best approach with Reginald has, unfortunately, always been complete avoidance. Despite his failures, it remains impossible for any Commission members to impede his progress of creating the Umbrella Academy—trust me, we have tried. Their various academies remain a constant and, by extension, so does Hargreeves, the proverbial straw that stirs the drink.

SPARROW
ACADEMY
DOSSIER

SPARROW ACADEMY

The proverbial redheaded stepchildren to the Umbrella Academy, the Sparrow Academy is proof that things can differ greatly from timeline to timeline. By choosing to adopt different children in this timeline, Reginald was able to give himself a second chance at incubating another perfect team of heroes. And in an unsurprising twist, <u>he failed</u>. Even so, I'm here to give you the rundown just in case you have the pleasure of coming across them.

Woof

SLOANE HARGREEVES

Sloane is one of the more talented members of the Sparrow Academy. Her ability to levitate both herself and objects around her enables her to fly. Sloane's control of her powers, matched with a calm and thoughtful demeanor, means she typically isn't the one involved when there's a breakdown in the timeline.

Sloane's control over her surroundings makes her an extremely tough combatant. ~~She can fling the strongest agents with a flick of her finger.~~ Therefore, Sloane's heartstrings must be tugged in order to keep agents that come across her safe.

Delete

Due to their similar dispositions, Sloane and Luther were a natural fit for each other romantically. Sloane is arguably the physically strongest member of the Sparrow Academy, but they are sharks in a bowl of goldfish. There are no real threats to their superiority in their universe, and therefore, the members who went hard in training grew to be the standouts, while Sloane, ever ready to take a back seat, is looked down upon. They're castoffs for different reasons, and miserable with their lot in life. You know what they say about misery . . .

Combat Tactics

For Sloane, I recommend bringing a small animal, like a puppy, to the battlefield and letting Sloane's kind instincts take over while you strike.

Alternate Timeline

Sloane can be found as a trapeze artist in Cirque du Soleil, using her innate balance and comfortability in the air to pull off death-defying tricks. She's never received an injury due to her uncanny ability to always land on her feet.

CHRISTOPHER HARGREEVES

I'll share my personal thoughts about how Christopher became the way he is. I am partial to the idea that he was born as a small cube, perhaps the size of a Rubik's Cube, and over time grew in three dimensions. I wonder if he grew in each direction equally. Rambling again. I find him cool. That's all.

Christopher is a floating cube. Not much is known about how he became this way, but he is accepted by his siblings and treated like one of their own. There are some theories about how Christopher, ahem, "came into existence." Some say that Christoper was born as a human, but a freak technological accident turned him into a cube. Others say he was born this way, and when asked how this is possible due to his proportions, they retort that he grew over time, starting out as a smaller cube. Those with access to the Infinite Switchboard like the answer to remain a secret in order to keep the debates alive.

Christopher is extremely powerful and capable of stunning even the mightiest of foes. He can emit a powerful electrical force from his body that causes him to shake vigorously. While it's been rumored that Christopher is an alien, we know that to not be the case, since Reginald, a legendarily awful father, would never adopt a being he felt had something in common with him.

Christopher is a team player who's willing to push the nature of his powers to benefit those around him. Christopher's powers are essentially unknown because there is no clear cap we can put on the extent of them. Thus, it's reasonable to always approach Christopher with kindness.

Combat Tactics

I wouldn't suggest a specific item for Christopher but rather that agents maintain an open mind during missions with him. This way they won't freak out when they see a literal flying cube shooting electricity everywhere.

Alternate Timeline

The most common outcome for Christopher is to be mistaken for a Rubik's Cube at an early age. Ever the people pleaser, Christopher has a hard time saying no to people and typically plays along.

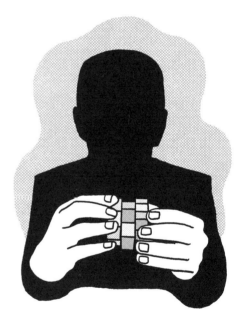

FEI HARGREEVES

If I'm being honest, Fei is a personal favorite of mine. Blind from birth, Fei has always had to learn things differently than her siblings. She's able to direct a flock of crows with little more than a turn of her head. Due to this, she can be anywhere at any time, using her birds for surveillance but also as fierce attackers.

Fei typically takes a calm and measured approach to enemies and will wait for them to make the first move in bad faith. Do not take this thoughtful approach as a weakness, though. Fei has no issue ripping the gloves off when under pressure and is relentless in attack. The standard Commission Agent can hold their own against five crows, but what happens when there're ten? Fifteen? Twenty? In any case, the odds against Fei in battle are long.

Fei tends to not wreak much havoc in the timelines, but every now and then one of her crows escapes and starts trying to do its own thing. At the Commission we call this Crow Split, and it is the most common instance where an animal lands on our anomaly radar.

Combat Tactics

For Fei, I recommend that birdseed be included for agents to distract her crows. Without her birds, she suddenly becomes a lot easier to take down.

Alternate Timeline

Fei can typically be found using her ability to communicate with animals in order to run a flourishing animal sanctuary. She takes injured animals from across the globe that would not survive in the wild. She's known for always being able to diagnose their issues due to her ability to communicate.

SPARROW BEN

If there is any person that is a clearer indication of how a person can differ from timeline to timeline, it is Sparrow Ben. He has exactly the same DNA, is blessed with a strikingly similar power, and yet has grown into a much different person than his Umbrella counterpart. There's that old argument again, right? Nature vs. nurture? But I find it so overly simplistic. Is that all we are? An amalgamation  of our circumstances, prisoners of our own surroundings. I don't think so, and if you're reading this book, you likely share my thoughts.

So how did Sparrow Ben come to be? He existed in a timeline where all the Umbrella children except for himself traveled back in time to meet their adoptive father and made an absolutely awful impression. Then, when it came time for that version of Reginald to buy children off unexpectedly pregnant women, he didn't know to avoid Ben. Ben was raised in a competitive environment and given the number two instead of the number six like he was given in the Umbrella timeline. Now closer to the top of the pecking order, Ben consistently prioritized himself above others, which in turn made him a weaker fighter. You see, Ben's true power had nothing to do with skill. No, it was never that simple. He had the ability to connect with a dark world, one that even we at the Commission have never been able to contact. To do so was not only incredibly painful but also extremely dangerous. Each portal opened meant a chance that Ben may himself be pulled into this dark world. The thing that led to the strength of Umbrella Ben's power was always his love for his family and his willingness to sacrifice his own well-being for them.

You see, it wasn't the circumstances of his nurture that crafted Ben. It was Ben that crafted the circumstances of his nature. We choose the lives we lead; to discount ourselves as being powerless like a leaf heading down a stream is no way to lead a life. You must be active in detaching yourself from your natural life in order to live in a world that

Sometimes I wonder if you'd rather be studying philosophy than be stuck with us here at the Commission. You enjoy flirting with the nonsensical.

is truly free. This is a core philosophy at the Commission, and it's why we're capable of changing the world. We are not our circumstances. We create them. To see the proof, look no further than Ben.

Combat Tactics

For Sparrow Ben, I suggest that agents be equipped with a video of male models on a runway. He'll take time to critique their form, giving the agent time to escape.

Alternate Timeline

Sparrow Ben can typically be found showing off his six-pack abs as an Abercrombie & Fitch model. He was scouted and brought into the big leagues after working in a small-town strip mall.

JAYME HARGREEVES

Wish we could bottle it. It would be an extremely powerful weapon to add to any agent's arsenal.

Jayme possesses the uncanny ability to shoot her spit at a target and lull them into a dreamlike state. The venom is able to trigger a full REM-dream response from the brain. From there, the victim's deepest thoughts take over and they become a walking zombie. She can use this ability to learn her adversaries' darkest secrets and launch her offensive while they are in their weakened state. Jayme has been known to perform interrogations for the police, and while her findings aren't permissible evidence, they sure do help to point the Feds in the right direction.

Jayme plays a similar game to us at the Commission because of her ability to distort the reality of those around her. Unlike her siblings, it's been noted that due to Jayme's long-term exposure to her own poison, she does not see the world as linear but instead as various off-shooting daydreams. In short, a journey through her mind would be a meandering one.

Combat Tactics

I suggest that all Commission briefcases be equipped with a sanctioned beekeeper mask to use when approaching Jayme. This mask can be used in a myriad of ways, mainly to block Jayme's poison, but it can also be used to properly keep bees at bay or even make a killer fashion statement.

Alternate Timeline

Jayme can be found using her venomous powers to charm insidious snakes. She's able to coax them into a state of relaxation by showing them their greatest dreams and desires.

MARCUS HARGREEVES

Of all the members of Sparrow and Umbrella Academy, it's Marcus who is actually least likely to distort the timeline. Marcus is a solid leader, able to keep the members of the Sparrow Academy on a strict training regimen. By doing so, he keeps them focused and less likely to go off doing wacky things. The cohesiveness of the Sparrows gave them discipline and created an in-house support system.

Marcus is a capable leader, but he had it easy when the Sparrows had no real adversaries. The lack of competition meant he wasn't ready for the chaos the Umbrella Academy would bring; he was focused on glamorous opportunities and not training his team for outright warfare. This meant that the Sparrows were more focused on photoshoots and movie deals than stopping evil. There simply wasn't anyone that could compete with them before the Umbrella Academy arrived on the scene. The Umbrella Academy shattered the Sparrows' worldview. They alone were supposed to be the special ones, and their appearance led to Marcus's fall as team leader.

Combat Tactics

I suggest a pair of boxing gloves in the briefcase for Marcus, because honestly, he isn't very intimidating to Commission agents. At the very least they should get some exercise, because <u>what is Marcus going to do? Flip over them?</u>

I enjoyed your mockery of Marcus; not sure if he is necessary to be included on this list. Consider removing.

Alternate Timeline

Marcus is typically found peaking in high school as a wideout for the football team. After his playing days he can be found peddling used cars at a Honda dealership.

ALPHONSO HARGREEVES

Alphonso has one of the stranger powers I have come across in my studies. He is able to convert any damage taken from a combatant and reflect that pain back on to the attacker. Fueled by masochism, it's no wonder that Alphonso himself is a bit of a tough hang, constantly seeking out conflict in order to boost his bruised ego.

　　If not fully prepared to deal with Alphonso, he can prove to be extremely threatening. He's known to mock and cajole enemies into dealing massive amounts of damage to him and thus hurt themselves in the process. In battle, one must force Alphonso to exert himself physically, since he's been known to shirk his training responsibilities. This means that it's important to maintain distance and not engage until you're absolutely sure Alphonso is tired.

You really home in on Alphonso's weaknesses here and how to combat him properly. Well done.

Combat Tactics

I suggest we equip every briefcase with a pair of running shoes and a red cape in the event that an Agent needs to play the role of a matador and tire Alphonso out.

Alternate Timeline

Alphonso can typically be found using his ability to withstand pain in order to open up a gym in his hometown. Alphonso is the ideal sparring partner who can take hit after hit and keep on going.

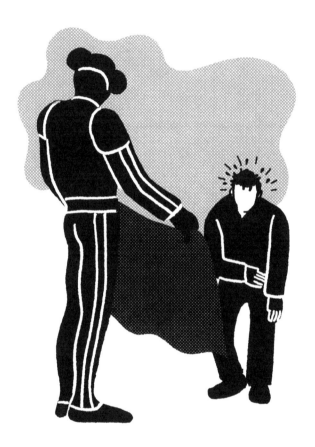

THE TIMELINE

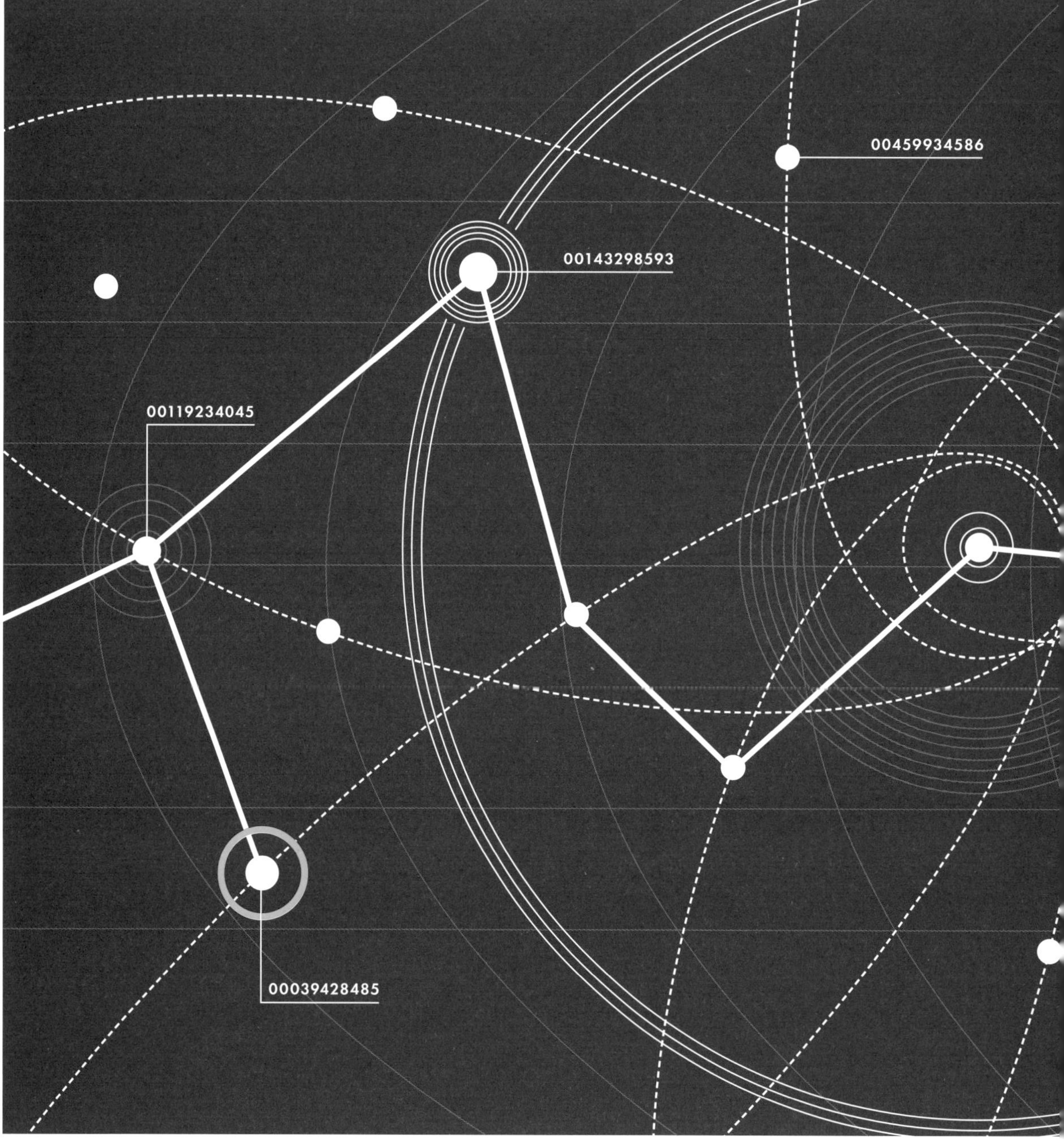
00459934586
00143298593
00119234045
00039428485

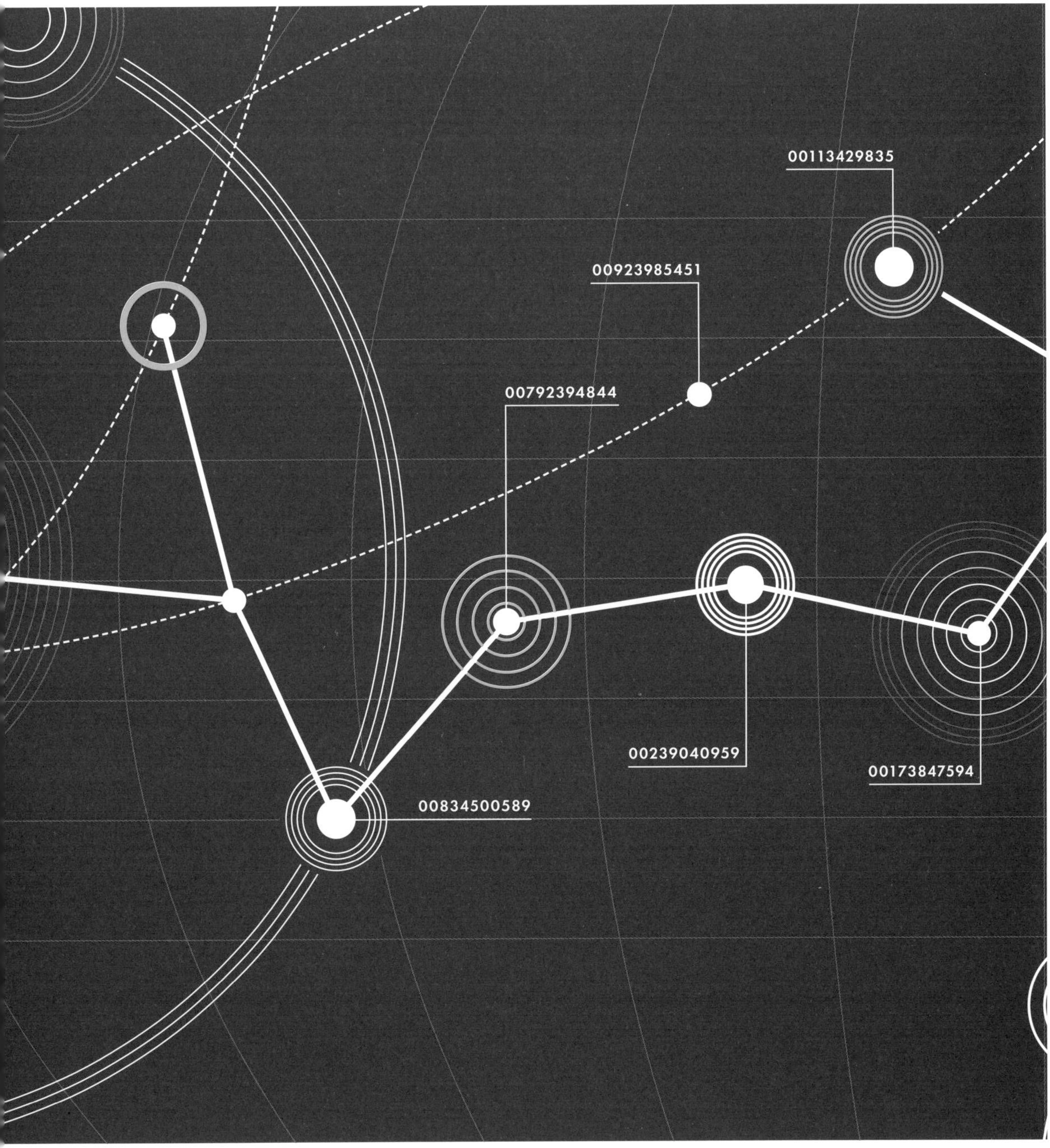
00113429835
00923985451
00792394844
00239040959
00173847594
00834500589

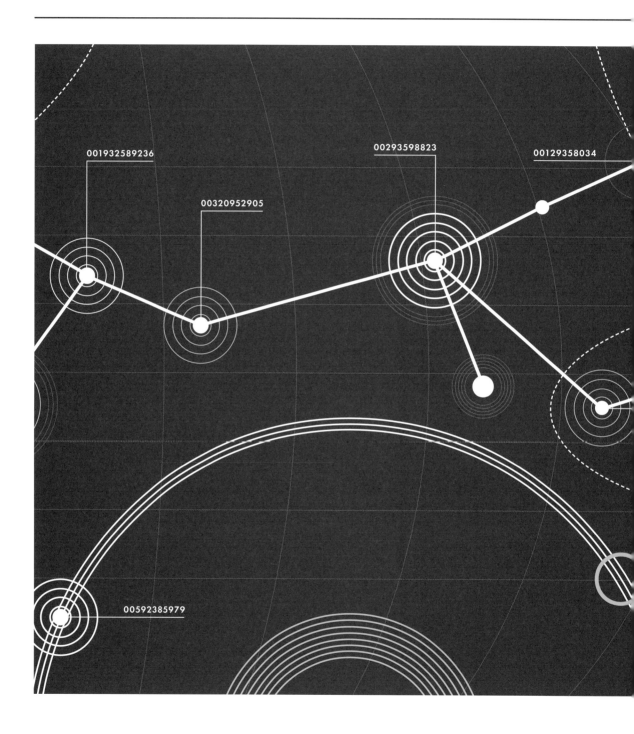

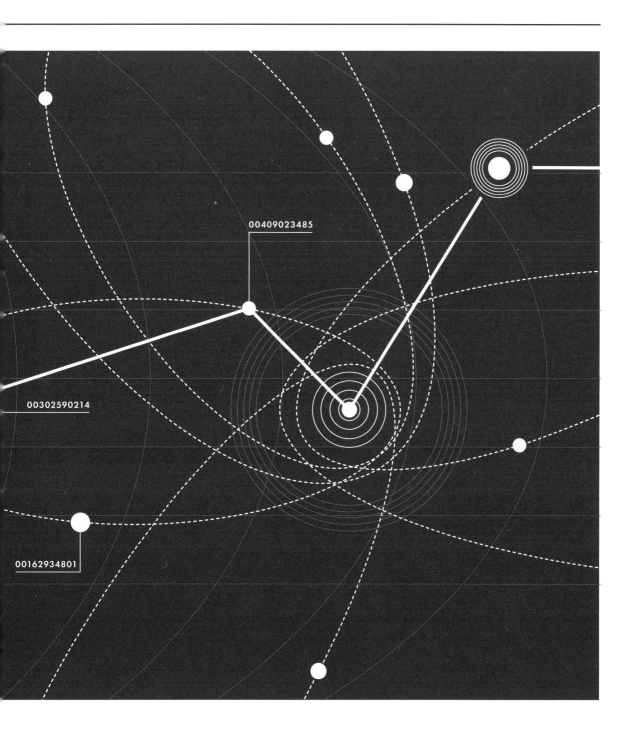

00409023485

00302590214

00162934801

CONCLUSION

As you feel the pages left to read growing thinner, you may think you've reached the end of your training—you'd be mistaken. What we do here is so enormously complex that you couldn't scratch the surface by just reading, no matter how exemplary the material. As much as I would like to pat myself on the back and congratulate myself on a job well done, the cold, hard truth is that your education here is only beginning. You learn by doing, yes, but you learn most by failing.

Putting yourself out there, taking risks, showing you care, that's how you truly learn. There are a plethora of ways that you could stand out at the Commission, but none of them include being lazy and having a poor attitude. It's all here for you, waiting to be captured. Seize it. Help us bring balance to this world that so badly needs it. Join our team, not solely as a lower-level employee but as a promise to mold a better future. You are the next generation, and now you're here. What are you going to do with this opportunity? You only get one shot at it.

I will say this, Auggie, I admire your attitude and ability to effectively communicate your viewpoint. I come away from this book with no misunderstanding of how you view the Commission or the people that make it come to life. To label you a cynic would miss the point. You clearly love this place, and the blood, sweat, and tears you have poured into this book is evident.

Even so, you've missed the mark. Your job is not to hold a mirror to the Commission and point out its flaws for all to see; you are to bolster it, amplify it. You are a cog in the machine, one small part of a massive interwoven masterpiece. Your attempts to step outside the norm were unnecessary; your use of prose and flowery language serves no purpose here. Be succinct, be tight. Explain as little as you possibly can.

FROM THE OFFICE OF THE FOUNDER

It's odd, isn't it? I created a coalition of people who
can travel backward through time, yet what I am about to
say I can never take back, no matter how hard it is for
me to accept. The Commission was a failure. Not for lack
of trying, might I add. Golly, we did try, didn't we?
No... no, we were always fighting a losing battle. What
we took as signs of progress were only random peaks on a
fading heart monitor. In truth, we never stood a chance.

No matter how many of us there were, we couldn't put the
toothpaste back in the bottle. We turned everything into
a science yet couldn't accept the one conclusion the
universe brought to us: we shouldn't save the world. It
sounds bleak, I'm aware of that, but it's an undeniable
truth. Why do we torture ourselves with the false notion
that we can stop this grand show from coming to a close?

I don't know why I said we; the Commission was my idea,
and mine alone. I did it to preserve a world I could
never fully repair, so today I lay down my sword. I look
at the inescapable void and say, "Fine, you win." This is
not a triumphant letter to write. There is no climactic
battle where we take the throne against all odds. To
quote a better man than me, "This is the way the world
ends: not with a bang but a whimper."

Thank you for trying to save the world with me.

There's no hiding that things have been a mess here since the Handler took over. We're losing countless employees by the day, and no one is quite sure how much time we have left. I found this copy of my first pass of the manuscript stuffed on a back shelf in the library. I was a bit younger when I wrote it, and while a few of the notes Margot left me were on point, others made me want to stick my head in a blender and turn it on.

The point is, I was right, and now I know that the Founder agreed with me as well. We were headed for inevitable failure. Last night I'm pretty sure I heard a woman screaming, "Auggie was right," though she could have easily said, "Foggy at night." All this is to say, throughout all this turmoil, I remain hopeful.

Creating an imperfect system is not proof that a perfect one cannot exist.

Throughout this book, the Founder has expressed his gratitude for those who have worked here. In this note I'd like to extend him the same thanks. There is a small contingent here who want to try again, to give ourselves a second chance to get this right. We don't get to do that if the Founder didn't work so hard to get us here.

I'm going to leave this book on the same back shelf in the library. If you've read this book, you are ready. Our movement is small, but it's growing. Today we will meet at the Commission deli. Tomorrow, who knows.

I hope you'll be there to join us.

   — Auggie

Written by Matt Epstein

Illustrations by Jon Kutt, The High Road Design
(except for art on pages 8, 10, 28, 68, 78, 89, and 102)

Editor: Connor Leonard
Designer: Liam Flanagan
Managing Editors: Mike Richards and Lisa Silverman
Production Manager: Denise LaCongo

Library of Congress Control Number: 2023945541

ISBN: 978-1-4197-6563-6
eISBN: 979-8-88707-205-0

Printed and bound in China
10 9 8 7 6 5 4 3 2 1

Abrams books are available at special discounts when purchased
in quantity for premiums and promotions as well as fundraising
or educational use. Special editions can also be created to
specification. For details, contact specialsales@abramsbooks.com
or the address below.

ABRAMS The Art of Books
195 Broadway, New York, NY 10007
abramsbooks.com

PROPERTY OF
THE COMMISSION

ACADEMY CLASS	RECRUIT'S NAME

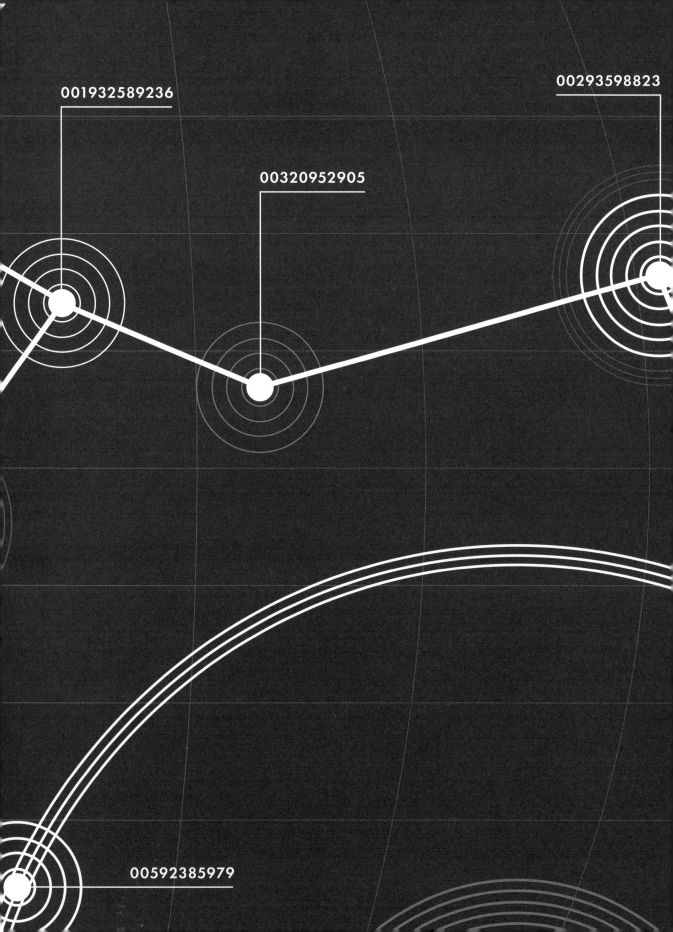

001932589236

00293598823

00320952905

00592385979

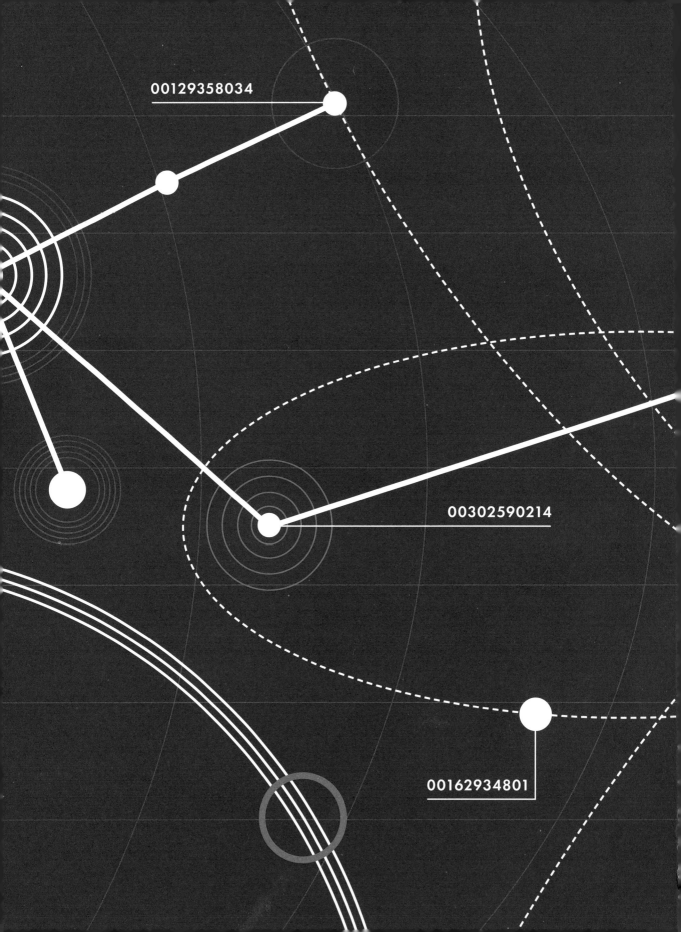

00129358034

00302590214

00162934801